The Teaching Techniques:

All pupils *must* complete either Dancing Bears Books A or Bear Necessities A1 and A2 before starting this book.

Although the beginning of Book A may seem very easy for pupils who have already made a start in reading, it is part of a carefully planned sequence.

1. **Using the flashcards**—it is not enough just to 'know' the letter-sounds. The response must be instant and automatic,. Practise the flashcards *every* lesson while using **Dancing Bears**!

2. **Using the cursor**—This is quite easy to learn. The cursor trains the child to read from left to right, and it trains them to look at every letter in a word.

3. **The 'Flashback Technique'**—After you have corrected an error, you must return to the same item again.

All this is explained on the following pages. Please read them carefully.

The Flashcards:

There are two sets of flashcards. The first set, printed on green card, were introduced in **Dancing Bears A**. Your pupil started learning the second set, printed on blue card, towards the end of **Book A** and the first three sounds are introduced on page 11. Some of the blue cards represent two phonemes (eg, 'oke' and 'ake'), but you will model these without breaking them down. All of the flashcards are numbered; it is important to teach them in order—the lowest number first.

Daily revision:

At the beginning of each lesson, go through all the cards in the front pocket. As the pupil gets each one right place it in a pile in front of them.

If they make a mistake or have forgotten a sound, use the **Flashback Technique**:

- tell your pupil the right sound,
- ask them to repeat it,
- slip the card behind the next one.

When the card comes up again they will almost certainly get it right and you will have converted an error into a success.

Shuffle the cards to mix up the order before you put them away.

Introducing a new sound:

If your pupil has made no more than two errors when going through the cards, you can introduce a new one.

- Pick out three flashcards that the pupil already knows well. They should not sound or look like the letter you are introducing—for instance, you would never use the letter /t/ when introducing /d/, or /n/ when introducing /u/.

- From the cards that your pupil does not know, pick out the one with the lowest number. You will work with these four cards.

- Hold up the new card and tell your pupil the sound, make sure they repeat it correctly. If they have a speech impediment, make sure that they pronounce it as they would in a word.

Dancing Bears

BOOK B

Hilary Burkard

& Tom Burkard

Stories illustrated by
Helen Dickson

First published 2001, Promethean Trust
Second Edition 2002, Promethean Trust
Third Edition (Revised) 2004, Hilary Burkard
Fourth Edition (Revised) 2005, Hilary Burkard
Fifth Edition (Revised) 2006, Hilary Burkard
Sixth Edition (Revised) 2013, Hilary Burkard
Seventh Edition (Revised) 2021, Hilary Burkard

ISBN: 9781905174454

PUBLISHED BY HILARY BURKARD

DISTRIBUTED BY
SOUND FOUNDATIONS
www.soundfoundations.co.uk
mckenzie@soundfoundations.co.uk

Dancing Bears B

Contents:

The Ground Rules:

The Sound Foundations philosophy:

As a teacher, your objective is to get your pupil to make the maximum number of correct responses—*and* the fewest errors—in the available time. If you manage to do this, you can't go far wrong.

1. **Teach—don't test.** Whenever a child gets stuck, say the sounds for them or tell them the word. Do not force them to 'work it out for themselves'. You do not want to make reading into a struggle.

2. Do not give ticks for a 'good try'. Just practise it and go back to it the next day.

3. Keep the lesson going at a cracking pace! Do not let your pupil's attention wander.

4. Daily lessons are essential. You only need to find 10 minutes per day for each slow reader.

- Slip the new card one card back. Show them the next card then put it to the back of the pack. The new card is now back on top. Repeat this a couple of times. Do this again, this time slipping the new card in two cards back each time it comes up. Your pupil has to remember it for a little bit longer. The old cards still go to the back each time. Repeat this a few times then finally put the new card at the back of the pack and go through the cards a couple of times more.

Your pupil may forget the new sound the next time you do your daily revision. However, by using the flashback technique, they will almost always start getting it right in a day or two—*it really is that easy!*

When do I stop using the flashcards?

When your pupil can say the sounds quicker than you can flip the flashcards then, unless they have not reached the page introducing that sound in the book, you can stop practising those cards. Do not be tempted to stop using the flashcards too soon. Your pupil must be able to respond instantly and automatically to the flashcards, otherwise, they will have trouble blending. You must practise 'past the point of perfection.' And no—your pupils will not get bored; children love getting it right!

Using the cursor:

The cursor is a piece of card about the size of a business card with a small notch cut out of one corner. You must use the cursor at all times.

- When your pupil is sounding out a word, you can reveal one sound at a time. For example, the word *shark* has three sounds—*sh...ar...k.*

- When your pupil already knows a word, just move the cursor smoothly and quickly across the letters. Never sound out words if you don't have to!

- If your pupil makes a mistake, you can back up the cursor and then sound out the word.

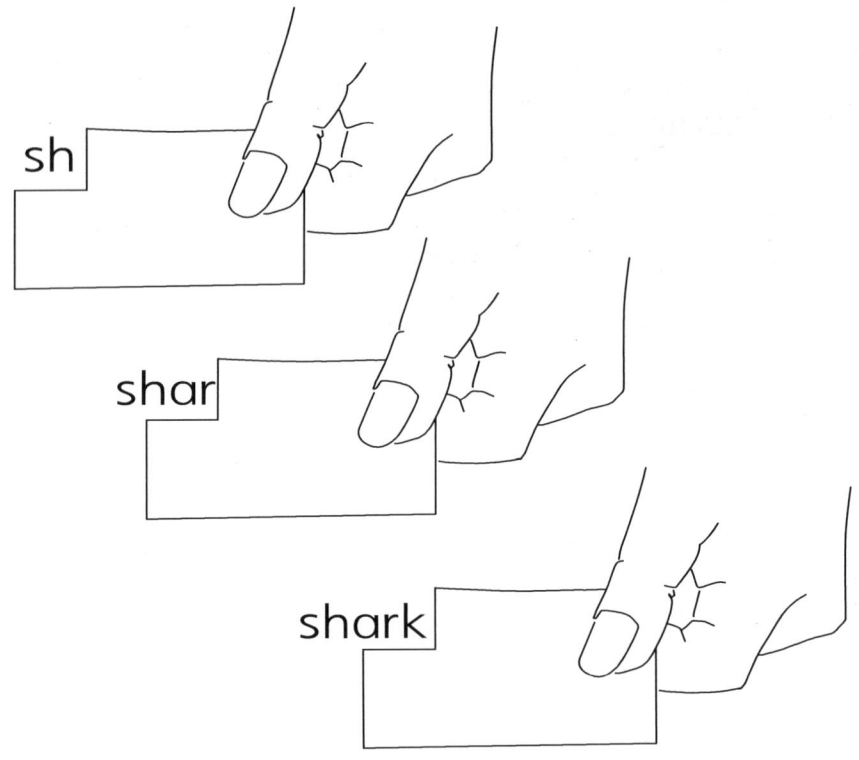

The cursor eliminates visual confusion. When children have been taught to read whole words, their eyes often jump all over the place, trying to scramble the letters to make a 'fit' with a word they know. If you use the cursor, it is highly unlikely that your pupil will need coloured overlays or tinted glasses.

The Flashback Technique:

Use the Flashback Technique every time your pupil makes an error. If you go back to the instructions for using the flashcards, you will see that when they have forgotten a card, you tell them what it is and then put it behind the next card. That way the card comes up again while it is still fresh in their memory. This is an example of the Flashback Technique.

You will also use the Flashback Technique when your pupil is reading words. Whenever they fail to read the word correctly:

• model the word,

• get them to repeat it,

• go on to the next item,

• go back to the one they just missed.

• When you have finished a line, go back again to any words missed.

• When you have finished the exercise for the day, go back over all the missed words again.

This way, your pupil will usually earn their tick for the line the next day. (Remember—you never tick a line when the pupil gets it right on the second go—you must wait until the next lesson.)

Comprehension:

The main purpose of this book is to teach decoding, but it is also important for pupils to extend their vocabulary, and to understand what they have read. The Cloze exercises require pupils to pay attention to meaning in order to identify the missing word, and the Word building pages present longer words in sentences, giving meaning through context. Our stories provide valuable decoding practice and improve reading fluency. Some of the words in the stories or Word builders may be unfamiliar to your pupil. If they ask the meaning of a word while reading, simply write it down where you see this symbol; ⌒⌒. You can also write down any new words here. Discuss their meanings briefly at the end of the lesson, and ask if your pupil can think of any **synonyms**—other words with the same meaning. At the start of the next lesson, quickly review these words to check that your pupil has retained their new vocabulary, (but never allow discussion of meaning to become a diversionary tactic to avoid reading practice!)

The Teaching Environment:

Always teach your pupil in a quiet room with no distractions. Do not let them bring toys or mobile phones with them.

Always sit facing your pupil. It is very difficult to use the cursor effectively if you are sitting side-by-side. You need eye contact. When you are facing your pupil it is easier to see when they are confused or getting tired. You can step in right away and show them what to do before they make a mistake and lose confidence.

Dancing Bears B

Affixes.

This is the first Decoding Sheet with words which are not pronounced as they are written. With most words that end in *-ed*, you do not pronounce the 'e'. The word *spelled* is pronounced *speld* or *spelt*.

When you add *-ed* to words that end in 'd' or 't', you **do** voice the 'e', but it is an unstressed *schwa* sound. In other words *needed* is pronounced *need'd*.

In later sheets, some words have a root which is not used on its own, for example: *disturb*. This is indicated by printing *turb* in italics.

Remember, if your pupil cannot read the word straight away, you **must** model it and get them to repeat it. Then go back to the word a few seconds later. *Never—ever—encourage a pupil to guess.*

-ing, -er, -all, -ly, -ed

If your pupil makes a mistake, back up the cursor and ound out the word.

sleep	sleeping	tall	taller	☐
quick	quickly	rest	rested	☐
go	going	short	shorter	☐
hard	hardly	ask	asked	☐
cry	crying	small	smaller	☐

Mark said that we must get going quickly. ☐

Now you have had a sleep, do you feel rested? ☐

Vern asked for a smaller bag of chips. ☐

The taller boy was hardly crying at all. ☐

Bart needs a shorter sleeping bag. ☐

fish	fishing	hard	harder	☐
rain	raining	start	started	☐
miss	missed	hang	hanging	☐
part	partly	munch	munched	☐

It has just started raining a lot harder. ☐

Do you think we should go fishing or flying? ☐

Ray missed the coat hanging on the back wall. ☐

Max munched on his pork chop all day. ☐

Decoding Power Pages:

These exercises are the 'secret ingredient' of **Dancing Bears**. All good readers can decode letters to sound, even if they have never seen the word before. This is how good readers learn new words.

When children read the words on the Decoding Power Pages, they should not be trying to find a 'match' with a word they know. All the words on Decoding Power Pages are regular—they can all be 'sounded out' without any guesswork. Some of the words are very unusual, like 'quern', 'bort' and 'loach'—but they are all real words.

Remember—you must always use the cursor. You must teach your pupils to scan from left to right, and to read every letter.

To earn a tick, the pupil must get all four words on a line right the first time. You may back up the cursor and tell them to 'try again', but you must not give any hints or prompts.

If your pupil cannot remember all the sounds or cannot blend them, say the sounds yourself and let them say the word. If they are in a total muddle, model the correct response. Always go back to any word you helped with—see **The Flashback Technique** on page 9.

DECODING ⚡ POWER ⚡ PAGE

Alweays use the cursor!

spot	plum	drab	grill	☐
tall	running	fitted	cutter	☐
bunk	end	fang	jolt	☐
hotly	wishing	fatter	helped	☐
coarse	steer	flair	score	☐
matted	quickly	fall	nipper	☐
stay	float	snail	spoil	☐
runner	hall	hitting	lastly	☐
breech	quest	horn	scorch	☐
landed	taller	flatly	calling	☐
erst	filth	snack	forth	☐
handed	partly	small	running	☐
sleet	crash	scar	keel	☐
ball	pinned	asking	zipper	☐

Dancing Bears B

Cloze Sentences:

Pupils enjoy these exercises and they get to practise using the words they have learnt by reading them in meaningful sentences.

In the box at the top of each page, you will find the new words that your pupil will need in order to read the sentences. Most are exception (tricky) words or words with ambiguous digraphs. Move the cursor smoothly across the letters while saying the sounds in the word. If your pupil gets confused, point out which sounds are regular and which are tricky. If they cannot read the word, model the correct response, then use the Flashback Technique (see page 9) and repeat each word until firm.

Reading the sentences:

For this exercise you will need a blank sheet of thin card about A6 in size. Cover the sentence and ask the pupil to read the three 'answer' words above the sentence first, using the cursor as usual. (This is to prevent them from guessing at the missing word.) Then let them read the sentence, still using the cursor. If the pupil reads the sentence and selects the right answer without prompting, circle the correct word. (The pupil **should not** write the word—this takes too long and is a distraction.) Otherwise, the sentence should be repeated in a subsequent lesson. If the pupil does not know the meaning of a word, explain it as simply as possible—but never encourage pupils to guess at words they have read incorrectly.

should, would, could, how, now, your

soft   sank   song

How long must we wait for the end of this ___?

pong   pond   pair

Last week, Max went fishing in your ___.

coal   coat   coast

Joan left her desk just now to get her ___.

bath   back   bunk

How did your car get a dent in the ___?

lung   pong   car

Your dog should not be left in the ___.

raining   boiling   sinking

Josh could not see the boat ___.

cost   cork   cart

How much did your posh hat ___?

quickly   hardly   partly

We must get going ___ or we could miss the train.

Fluency Reading:

Timed readings will help your pupil read words quickly and automatically. At first, the times are very generous and most pupils will find them easy to acheive. However, some children get nervous when they are being tested, and you do not want them to be worried by the stopwatch. For real timing-phobics, sit the child with their back to a wall clock with a second hand.

Frame the first word in the line with the cursor, and then say 'go'. Move the cursor as fast as the pupil can read. Record the time on the sheet and tick the line off if the pupil reads every word within 10 seconds. The usual rules apply—if your pupil makes a mistake, you can move the cursor back and let them have another go but you cannot give them any help. Model any word they get stuck on and re-time that line the next day.

Unless our pupil is extremely slow, they will want to try for bonus points. You can award one bonus point if they read the line in 8 seconds, and two bonus points if they read it in 6 seconds. Motivate your pupil with rewards when they get enough points. If your pupil wants to have another go at a line, they must wait until the following day.

Story:

The purpose of the story is to provide decoding practice and to improve reading fluency, but you should always check your pupil's comprehension, and, at the end of the lesson, briefly discuss the meaning of any new or unfamiliar words. Write these down where you see this symbol: ⌒.

There are no tick-boxes for this exercise but, if your pupil struggles with a sentence, they should be encouraged to read it again. If their reading is very hesitant, it may be a good idea to read the story twice to improve fluency and comprehension. Model any words on which the pupil gets stuck.

FLUENCY READING

part	mitt	that	rush	☐ ☆ ☆
fad	than	posh	moss	☐ ☆ ☆
deck	mash	bid	tick	☐ ☆ ☆
bark	luff	with	been	☐ ☆ ☆
con	thin	deep	fen	☐ ☆ ☆
duck	sheep	Jess	nerd	☐ ☆ ☆
sham	gob	Serb	far	☐ ☆ ☆
buff	buck	fee	nag	☐ ☆ ☆
bath	dish	tod	puck	☐ ☆ ☆
peel	ness	sock	shot	☐ ☆ ☆
teg	herb	seem	duff	☐ ☆ ☆
berth	arm	bin	them	☐ ☆ ☆
feet	doff	kick	card	☐ ☆ ☆

Groan, the Croaking Toad.

Vern, Bart and Froid rested by the stairs in Bart's shack. Groyne, the grey-green goat, who wore his hair in a quiff, munched on some foil by the oak board. Groyne looked at Mark, who now wore a ragged shirt with sleeves a yard long, baggy shorts and pink flip-flops that were as big as boats.

"You look like a mix of Meg's Mum and Dad," said Groyne.

"That shirt would fit a tall man and your shorts need a belt to keep them up." said Vern. "Your Mum will be so mad if sees you, you could be a tramp. She will think you are not her smart Mark. Are those long shorts you have got on, or short longs? Ha, ha, ha!"

"But I am her Mark," said Mark, "I am a boy who is six. I need some lunch and I need to find a store." He had to get a shirt and some shorts so his Mum would think he was her smart boy and not be cross. He left Bart's shack to see if he could find a store for shorts and shirts. He left Herb, the sharp shark, who was sleeping on his back with his bus pass stuck in his fin. He went past the hill of moist muck quickly, but just as he saw Groan, the croaking toad, his shorts fell to his shins, he tripped over his pink flip-flops and he slipped on some wet mud.

18

"Where were you going so fast and why are you crying?" croaked Groan.

Mark said, "I am crying for I need some lunch and I must find a smart shirt and a pair of shorts that fit."

Groan said, "Well, I sell all sorts of shorts and shirts. Come to my store now and you will find shirts and shorts for smaller boys. We have red shirts and green shorts. We have sharp shirts for shorter chaps, and we sell smart shorts for tall boys. We may have flip-flops that fit as well, unless you would like some trainers? This is the best store in the dump."

should, would, could, how, now, your

chimp   coin   chair

Could you hang your vest on the back of the ___?

damp   desk   dump

Should we tip this junk in the ___?

hank   hand   help

Your dog sank his fangs into my left ___!

shell   shelf   shall

Would you jump up and get that lamp off the top ___?

vests   vents   vans

Would you mend my best silk ___?

bunk   bank   back

Now you are big you should not thump him ___.

desk   dent   dump

If you bump into my car you must pay for mending the ___.

coal   coil   cost

Could you send a boy to ask how much that lamp ___?

-es, -est, -ful, -less, -en, -y

If your pupil makes a mistake, back up the cursor and sound out the word.

glass	glasses	strong	strongest	☐
fall	fallen	smell	smelly	☐
box	boxes	rot	rotten	☐
stick	sticky	small	smallest	☐
get	getting	rust	rusty	☐

You must pack the glasses in the strongest boxes. ☐

The fallen trees blocked the road. ☐

The smallest car is getting a bit rusty. ☐

The rotten pork was sticky and smelly ☐

tall	tallest	horse	horses	☐
feel	feeling	play	playful	☐
greed	greedy	luck	lucky	☐
thank	thankful	cord	cordless	☐
help	helpful	block	blocked	☐

The tallest horses are feeling playful. ☐

My dad is helpful with his cordless drill. ☐

You should be thankful that you are so lucky. ☐

Do not be so greedy or they will not feed you. ☐

DECODING ⚡ POWER ⚡ PAGE

Do not award ticks for a 'good try'—your pupil will pay for it later!.

costly	tapped	landing	harder	☐
rotten	tallest	foxes	happy	☐
hoarse	flair	adore	sneer	☐
handful	harmless	fatten	dotty	☐
stoat	hoist	quaint	stern	☐
horses	playful	smallest	spotless	☐
helper	rubbed	badly	falling	☐
brash	steep	float	scar	☐
sunken	hottest	musty	glasses	☐
score	queer	hair	oar	☐
gleeful	sharpen	feckless	sticky	☐
quitting	boxer	sorted	deftly	☐
clash	creel	broth	slain	☐
bosses	fattest	helpful	thicken	☐

very, many, any, one, none, done

damp   dad   darn

Did Gail send very many gifts to her ___?

shaft   shank   shelf

Are Meg's pink shirts up on the top ___?

lunch   lump   lamp

Has anyone rung the bell for __?

bang   bank   band

Could your mum get any cash from the ___?

roach   road   roast

There are not many trucks on this ___.

dress   drip   drag

My gran has a black ___.

your   yard   yarn

They will clamp any cars that park in that ___.

songs   sharks   socks

None of my ___ are very smelly.

FLUENCY READING

will	dock	shell	fib	☐ ☆ ★
her	carp	cox	ruck	☐ ☆ ★
lash	fid	then	seed	☐ ☆ ★
fern	quack	jar	lag	☐ ☆ ★
verb	queen	heel	cos	☐ ☆ ★
York	moth	fork	bash	☐ ☆ ★
rid	thug	North	art	☐ ☆ ★
god	larch	thick	quit	☐ ☆ ★
lee	wit	path	chock	☐ ☆ ★
nib	quiz	pack	much	☐ ☆ ★
shin	bob	wack	torn	☐ ☆ ★
park	ten	porch	quick	☐ ☆ ★
Dick	bar	quid	Jack	☐ ☆ ★

Hank, the Hunch-Backed Horse.

Mark missed Vern and his pet snail, Froid. He had to get some shorts, a shirt and smart trainers that fit from Groan's store. He went into the store, where he saw stacks of shorts and many hanging shirts. He saw green and red dresses for girls, and boxes of the smallest coats for kids.

Groan croaked, "Here are some smashing shirts for fishing, and some keen shorts for marching. Pick any one and try it on. But do not drop them in the muck, or you will spoil them."

Mark put on some boy's green shorts, a red shirt that was not very long, and some black trainers that fit. "How much must I pay for this?" he asked.

Groan croaked, "For you my pal, that will be ten quid if you can pay now."

Mark said, "But I just have six quid, and I still must get a loaf and some milk for my Mum."

Groan croaked, "That is very sad, but I cannot sell one shirt at a loss. You must go and get some more cash."

So, Mark left Groan's store to get some more cash. He could not ask his pals for any, they would just think he was begging, and they would give him none. Mark marched into the moist muck, and then he met Hank, the hunch-backed horse.

"Who are you? Where did you come from? Why are you crying? How did you get here?" Hank asked.

"I am Mark and I need some cash to get a pair of shorts and a shirt, so that my Mum and my pals will think I am smart" Mark said.

"Why would you want them to think you are smart? I can see you are not, with your big, ragged shirt, pink flip-flops and long shorts—or are they short longs? You should not try to trick Mum and your pals." said Hank. Mark just started crying harder.

| very, many, any, one, none, done |

jail   join   jar

Did Beth get any sticky sweets from the ___?

coin   class   clap

There are not very many boys in this ___.

drink   drop   drag

Did anyone see where she put her ___?

pink   past   pond

One of the sailing boats sank in the ___.

shell   shelf   smack

How many glasses are on the top ___?

set   said   spilt

None of them has done the task they were ___.

barn   boat   bill

Joy still has not paid the ___.

painting   boiling   flying

Jack has done a big ___ of us all.

Mastery Test

If your pupil does not pass this test, they must go back to page 11. This is very important—a child who is struggling will not be learning. Contrary to what you would think, most children would rather go back than carry on getting things wrong. If your pupil needs to go back, use a different coloured pencil for ticking the boxes.

Use the cursor as you would on a Fluency Reading page.

Timed reading: 'Pass' mark is 15 seconds per line.

trying	coach	snore	slay	☐
sheer	harder	champ	twig	☐
nerd	noise	frail	quickly	☐
foxes	happy	quilt	started	☐

Reading accuracy: Pass mark is one mistake.
Do not prompt. You may allow the pupil to self correct, but you cannot say anything except "Try again".

I think we should get going now.　☐

Herb handed me the smallest snail.　☐

The farmer was very helpful.　☐

All of your glasses are still very sticky.　☐

28

-ke Endings:

Your pupil will already be familiar with words such as *give* and *horse* where the final 'e' is silent. The next page is the first introduction to the Split Digraph or Magic 'e' Rule. Do not start this sheet if your pupil has not mastered the advanced flashcards numbered 4 – 8. Make sure you reveal both parts of the digraph together with the cursor.

Some pupils have trouble getting used to these words and forget that the final 'e' makes the preceding vowel long.

If your pupil is struggling you can do one of two things: You can reverse the cursor so your pupil just sees the same ending as on the relevant flashcard—e.g. 'ake'. If they say it correctly, then take away the cursor and let them read the word.

Alternatively, you can take them through the Split Digraph Rule.

The Split Digraph Rule:

Point to the final 'e' and ask "What letter does this word end with?" Then point to the vowel and say "What is the *name* of this letter?" Then tell them "In this word, the 'e' makes the vowel say its own name.

You may have to say the sounds yourself (as in oral blending) and then ask the pupil to say the word.

If you pupil is confused by long 'u' words where the vowel is pronouced like the 'oo' in *m<u>oo</u>n*, model the word and ask him to repeat it. Use the Flashback Technique to reinforce the correction.

-ake, -eke, -ike, -oke, -uke

Remember to practise the flashcards at least once a day!

bake	cake	pike	strike	snake	☐
fake	brakes	bike	take	like	☐
quake	hike	shake	rake	Mike	☐

Did Gail bake a fresh cake? ☐

Do you think a pike will strike at my bait? ☐

Is that stuffed snake a fake? ☐

I would like to take you on a hike to the farm. ☐

A quake can shake things up a bit. ☐

My brakes stop my bike very quickly. ☐

take	trike	drake	like	lake	☐
Mike	wake	spike	sake	Jake	☐
flake	bike	stake	make	pike	☐

Mike hit the brass spike into the wall. ☐

For my sake, you should not wake me so quickly. ☐

Can Jake make a stake from this chunk of oak? ☐

If you hit a flint with steel, it will chip off a flake. ☐

Can I take my trike to the shop? ☐

Drakes and ducks like to swim on this lake. ☐

DECODING ⚡ POWER ⚡ PAGE

Always use the cursor!

helpless	fallen	smelly	wishes	☐
like	truck	duke	fake	☐
gall	telling	flatter	mended	☐
back	hike	puke	woke	☐
board	queer	snore	stair	☐
yuck	stoke	lake	bike	☐
playful	happen	luckless	thinnest	☐
brim	skip	twit	flip	☐
Peke	Jack	spoke	brick	☐
hardly	stall	quacking	bloater	☐
hake	nick	moke	luck	☐
mucky	wilful	bitten	backless	☐
faint	spoilt	sport	twerp	☐
loke	Jake	pick	spike	☐

very,	many,	any,	one,	none,	done

prong   trunk   pond

There are not very many green frogs in that ___.

track   truck   trick

How many drums of black oil fell from the back of the ___?

plums   plugs   prams

Would you give me one of your sweet ___?

grid   gran   grass

Did you ask for a very big gift from your ___?

hilt   help   hill

Are there any black sheep left on the ___?

jump   jail   jam

Sam just had one drink, but they still put him in ___.

jay   joy   jug

Is there any water left in the ___?

swim   queen   sweet

The smell of fresh cut grass is very ___.

FLUENCY READING

cuff	worn	tern	feed	☐ ☆ ★
rich	kerb	seen	porch	☐ ☆ ★
perm	bod	chap	pith	☐ ☆ ★
cart	sort	Thor	rash	☐ ☆ ★
quiff	teeth	hem	quint	☐ ☆ ★
lick	shun	charm	Perth	☐ ☆ ★
darn	forth	thorp	nub	☐ ☆ ★
nor	chuck	mark	weep	☐ ☆ ★
boy	goth	tort	road	☐ ☆ ★
nosh	berg	goat	chick	☐ ☆ ★
shim	coat	hers	quill	☐ ☆ ★
join	lard	hack	boil	☐ ☆ ★
quell	weed	day	shock	☐ ☆ ★

Jake, the Fake Snake.

Hank, the hunch-backed horse, saw that Mark was crying and he felt bad. How could he help? Mark needed someone to help him to find some more cash so that he could get a pair of shorts that fit, a shirt, and some smart trainers from Groan's store. He needed to find ten quid to pay Groan the croaking toad.

Hank said, "Horses do not have any cash, but I wish I could help you. I can take you to see Jake, the fake snake, who is very helpful too. You will like Jake"

Mark said, "I would like that very much. I would like to be smart again. If I can not get some cash from someone, I am done." So, Hank and Mark went off to see Jake, the fake snake.

"Jake lives at the far end of the tip." Hank said, "If anyone can tell you how to get some coins to pay for a shirt, some shorts and a pair of trainers, it is Jake."

On the way from the hill of moist muck they had to take a path that went by a lake. They saw many ducks and drakes on the lake. They saw a drake flying back to Bart's shack and Mark wished he was with Vern and Froid, the pet snail.

"I wish I had a bike," he said.

"You would just get stuck in the mud if you had a bike." said Hank the hunch-backed horse.

At last, they got to the marsh where Jake, the fake snake, lived.

"Why do they call Jake a fake snake?" asked Mark.

want, watch, walk, water, wash, above, love

grin   glad   gran

Jake should wash that dark green dress for his___.

take   track   tail

The train struck a tree trunk that fell on the ___.

want   water   walk

Spike acted swiftly to stop the boy from jumping in the ___.

walk   wind   wisp

Any tall shrub or tree will sway in a strong ___.

drip   drain   drink

I saw where Mike put your ___ of water.

joy   jest   job

I think they just want to get that ___ done.

watching   walking   wanting

Jake loves to go ___ in the hills.

water   watch   wash

I would love to fly above the ___.

-ake, -eke, -ike, -oke, -uke

If your pupil makes a mistake, back up the cursor and sound out the word.

stroke	likes	smoke	Coke	Luke	☐
broke	duke	spoke	Jake	poke	☐
Mike	wake	bike	joke	bloke	☐

You may tell a joke if it is very funny. ☐

Take this can of Coke to Jake, he is sitting by the lake ☐

That bloke likes to have a smoke with his beer. ☐

The Duke spoke to Luke just now. ☐

Jake will wake up if you poke him in the ribs. ☐

I think Mike broke his bike chain. ☐

Luke	woke	spike	stoke	choke	☐
smoke	like	Coke	pike	take	☐
bloke	nuke	lake	rake	fluke	☐

Luke woke up at six o'clock. ☐

Spike went on a trip to Stoke-on-Trent last week. ☐

It was just a fluke that the smoke woke Mike. ☐

You should take the rake and a digging fork. ☐

As I am broke, would you pay for my glass of Coke? ☐

She would like to fish for pike in the lake. ☐

37

DECODING ⚡ POWER ⚡ PAGE

Some of these words are unusual but they are all real words.

fastest	sticky	torches	bashful	☐
hick	fluke	snake	pike	☐
needed	fairly	call	parting	☐
neck	track	stake	yoke	☐
store	cheer	hoard	bairn	☐
kick	make	Luke	stuck	☐
sweeten	chinless	thickest	tricky	☐
band	lend	runt	link	☐
poke	bake	chick	quake	☐
sweeper	railed	softly	ball	☐
muck	brick	slick	eke	☐
classes	wishful	chicken	helpless	☐
twain	gloat	joist	green	☐
quack	nuke	bloke	Dick	☐

want, watch, walk, water, wash, above, love

batter   baited   badly

The black cloak fitted her ___.

press   dress   desk

The zipper on my ___ got stuck.

shopping   shipping   slipping

Beth was just saying how much she wanted to go ___.

shutter   butter   summer

It can get very hot in ___.

hamper   hammer   handed

I keep hitting my hand with the ___.

dinner   digger   dipper

Gus was so fat that he hardly needed his ___.

shopping   selling   sailing

I want to watch the boats ___.

mainly   thickly   skipper

Kay coated her cracker with cheese very ___.

FLUENCY READING

perch	toy	beet	perk	☐ ☆ ★
pain	torch	darn	rain	☐ ☆ ★
chill	chub	mail	marsh	☐ ☆ ★
thorn	ray	ford	say	☐ ☆ ★
horse	rack	paid	arch	☐ ☆ ★
ash	way	quill	Bert	☐ ☆ ★
pail	parch	verse	oath	☐ ☆ ★
form	eel	void	orb	☐ ☆ ★
nerve	boat	norm	lath	☐ ☆ ★
loin	quiff	mesh	toad	☐ ☆ ★
leech	hock	joy	quip	☐ ☆ ★
thud	hay	morse	reed	☐ ☆ ★
coy	fort	thick	vain	☐ ☆ ★

my + self = myself

At the Creepy Marsh.

Jake, the fake snake, lived in the creepy marsh at the far end of the tip. He stayed in a rusty car that had been left to rot in the dump.

"How do you do?" said Jake, who was very well-bred, "Take a chair and take a load off your feet. Would you like a drink?" Mark sat in a dusty chair, but it sank into the muck very quickly.

"Could I have a glass of milk?" he asked.

Jake said, "This is not your lucky day, for I just have oat milk."

Hank, the hunch-backed horse, asked, "Do you make your milk with oats? Horses like oats but do they make good milk?" Jake, the fake snake, got some oat milk from a rusty car, but Mark could not drink much of it, for it was very thick and sweet.

He asked, "Why do they call you a fake snake?"

Jake said, "You see I have ten feet and six hands. Snakes do not have hands and feet."

Then Hank, the hunch-backed horse, said, "My pal, Mark, needs your help. He needs to get some cash so that he can get a pair of shorts and a shirt, and some smart trainers from Groan, the croaking toad. How can he get some cash?"

Jake, the fake snake, hissed sharply. "It is very hard to find cash in this dump," he said, "I have none myself. You could go to see Mike, the greedy loan shark. He lives next to Luke, the Duke of the dump. If you set off from here now, you can get there by dark—but it may take longer in flip-flops."

Mastery Test

If your pupil does not pass this test they must go back to page 30. This is very important—a child who is struggling will not be learning. Contrary to what you would think, most children would rather go back than carry on getting things wrong. If your pupil needs to go back, use a different coloured pencil for ticking the boxes.

Use the cursor as you would on a Fluency Reading page.

Timed reading: 'Pass' mark is 15 seconds per line.

spotless	fair	sweeper	spoke	☐
sharpen	wake	boiled	twerp	☐
sailing	hoard	rusty	pike	☐
fluke	gloat	queer	boxes	☐

Reading accuracy: Pass mark is one mistake.
Do not prompt. You may allow your pupil to self correct, but you cannot say anything except "Try again".

Did Jake take his bike to go shopping? ☐

Mike drank the last of his Coke quickly. ☐

Luke will not like all that smelly smoke very much. ☐

Spike needed the cordless drill to get one of his jobs done. ☐

want, watch, walk, water, wash, above, love

rubbing   ratting   raining

All the players stopped playing ball when it started ___.

junk   jump   jam

The digger loaded the skip with ___.

hill   hail   hull

All the tall men and small boys are walking up the ___.

duck   dock   dark

They are watching the sailing boat landing at the ___.

drink   block   dress

My mum is mixing soap in hot water so she can wash her silk ___.

bunk   bigger   ball

Luke was going to watch the batter hitting the ___.

pluck   play   pall

Come quickly and you can watch the band ___.

weld   walk   water

I think you should ___ the dog.

re-, be-, un-, ex-, pre-, dis-

If your pupil makes a mistake, back up the cursor and sound out the word.

less	unless	port	report	☐
plain	explain	load	unload	☐
float	refloat	fore	before	☐
dress	undress	*rupt*	disrupt	☐

Luke will not let us go unless we unload the car. ☐

Could you explain why you got such a bad report? ☐

The divers had to refloat the sunken ship. ☐

We must undress before we go to bed. ☐

If you make a noise, you will disrupt Luke's sleep. ☐

tend	pretend	tract	distract	☐
cuss	discuss	mark	remark	☐
pay	repay	vent	prevent	☐
gust	disgust	well	unwell	☐

Did you discuss that smart remark with Joan? ☐

Do not distract Mike if he is trying to fix the car. ☐

Spike has to repay that loan before the week-end. ☐

Will the smell of rotten fish disgust Jake? ☐

If you do not want to go, pretend to be unwell. ☐

DECODING ⚡ POWER ⚡ PAGE

Do not award ticks for a 'good try'—your pupil will pay for it later!

clack	broke	drake	Mike	☐
replay	before	unpick	expel	☐
sharpest	soapy	boxes	thankful	☐
predict	disdain	refund	between	☐
wall	hoarding	fairer	joined	☐
unseen	explore	prevail	distress	☐
wake	suck	juke	choke	☐
aboard	flair	shore	jeer	☐
resent	beset	unfit	express	☐
batten	aimless	daftest	rainy	☐
pretend	dismiss	reject	before	☐
hack	joke	pluck	shake	☐
joint	frail	coast	steep	☐
unjust	explain	prevent	distort	☐

> want, watch, walk, water, wash, above, love

hall   have   ham

Could you hang up your coat in the ___?

drink   drain   branch

Your dad is boiling some water for a hot ___.

hanger   hopper   hammer

I want to watch you bang in the nail with the ___?

tamp   tall   task

My mum is six feet ___.

swings   swigs   sweets

Who is paying for all the ___?

quacking   clucking   quickly

Luke said he wanted me to walk ___.

pond   port   pork

We got in a big digger to deepen the ___.

band   boast   boat

I love to go sailing in my ___.

FLUENCY READING

☐ Pass: 10 sec.   ☆ Bonus: 8 sec.   ★ Double Bonus: 6 sec.

beer	lark	foil	hair	☐ ☆ ★
pert	fail	sore	cord	☐ ☆ ★
soap	more	jeep	goal	☐ ☆ ★
wore	mock	coach	pair	☐ ☆ ★
beech	coin	fair	harsh	☐ ☆ ★
may	cheer	terse	pay	☐ ☆ ★
jeer	quack	bay	roar	☐ ☆ ★
shut	Roy	board	chock	☐ ☆ ★
toil	hoard	march	chore	☐ ☆ ★
quern	bait	morn	reel	☐ ☆ ★
pore	check	tail	cork	☐ ☆ ★
seer	thick	foam	queen	☐ ☆ ★
marl	jeer	herd	day	☐ ☆ ★

48

Hank Feels Unwell.

Hank, the hunch-backed horse, said, "I was too greedy. I drank much more of the sweet oat milk than I should have and now I feel unwell. I want some water for a wash."

Jake, the fake snake, said, "If you can walk to my bath, you can wash your hands and feet in hot water."

"But horses do not have hands and feet," said Hank. Then he was sick in the marsh and fell asleep with a crash.

Mark wanted to start walking up the road to find Mike, the loan shark, for he needed some cash to pay for a pair of shorts and a shirt and some trainers. He wanted to look smart to see his pals, Vern and Froid. He wanted to see Bart, the junk yard dog, too. He missed the smell of damp dog.

"Who can take me to see Mike, the loan shark?" said Mark, "I do not know the way and I do not want to get lost."

Jake, the fake snake, said, "I would love to help you, but I need socks and trainers just like you. I need ten socks and ten trainers, for I have ten feet. I am missing one of my trainers. I will toss a pail of water on Hank and he will wake up."

Hank did get up and had to shake the water from his hair. He said, "Why, we must march on. We must not slip on the slushy trail that takes us to see Mike, the loan shark. I will not let my pal fail."

So they left Jake, the fake snake, who lived in a rusty car by the creepy marsh. They walked up the slushy trail that went by the reedy lake.

"Unless we are quick, it will get dark before we find Mike, the loan shark," said Hank. Then he slipped on some sloppy mud and fell into a yucky pond.

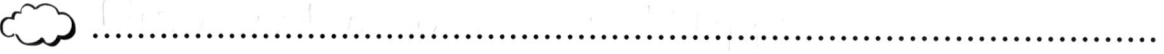

-igh, -tch, -dge

hitch	lodge	fridge	night	edge	☐
ditch	light	switch	dredge	sludge	☐
catch	bridge	high	pitch	smudge	☐
bright	match	badge	notch	might	☐

Could Mike hitch a lift to the lodge? ☐

I like to raid the fridge at night. ☐

Do not stand on the edge of the ditch. ☐

You must switch off the lights at night. ☐

Did they dredge the sludge from the lake? ☐

right	judge	twitch	fetch	thigh	☐
stretch	scotch	midge	blight	clutch	☐
patch	slight	budge	sketch	fight	☐
fudge	itch	fright	dodge	sigh	☐

My dad asked me to fetch his glass of scotch. ☐

I have a slight twitch in my thigh. ☐

You will get a red blotch where the midge bit you. ☐

The judge said we should go right at the lights. ☐

Who trimmed that stretch of hedge? ☐

DECODING ⚡ POWER ⚡ PAGE

Always use the cursor!

refrain	begin	unstuck	exact	☐
catch	hedge	night	ditch	☐
quick	rake	smoke	eke	☐
judge	high	fetch	badge	☐
marches	needful	often	thankless	☐
etch	lodge	right	hatch	☐
prevent	display	reset	betray	☐
coyly	all	failing	thinner	☐
fridge	light	pitch	nudge	☐
flake	Luke	puck	shack	☐
tight	batch	ridge	fight	☐
unwell	expand	prefix	disrupt	☐
Ray	point	croak	fleet	☐
itch	fudge	sight	thatch	☐

Word building:

Most pupils like these exercises because they discover that reading long words is not really all that difficult, once you know the building blocks, or 'morphemes'.

Most of the examples start off with a real word but there are some that start with a part of a word such as *cept* or *struct*. These are always in italics. Some morphemes have more than one syllable.

The only difficult items are the ones where the syllable structure changes in the middle of the line, these are marked with a star in the exercises. For instance:

late　　relate　*relative　relatively

Note that in speech, 'relate' breaks up as *re-late,* whereas 'relative'

works out as *rel-uh-tive*. With words like this, you will probably have to tell your pupil the correct response the first time round. Do not forget to use the Flashback Technique.

With the cursor, segment the root word into phonemes as usual. Then with each successive word use the cursor to reveal each morpheme as a whole.

Comprehension:

At the end of the lesson, check your pupil's comprehension of any new or unfamiliar words. Write these down where you see this symbol; ⌒, and briefly discuss the meanings.

Wordbuilder

load	reload	reloaded		☐
tend	pretend	pretending		☐
gust	disgust	disgusting		☐
long	belong	belonging	belongings	☐

The hunter reloaded his gun. ☐

Jake was just pretending that he was broke. ☐

Mike's dog smells very disgusting tonight. ☐

You must take all of your belongings with you. ☐

dress	undress	undressing	☐
part	depart	departed	☐
bid	forbid	forbidden	☐
press	express	expressly	☐
tract	distract	distracted	☐

I was undressing so that I could have a wash. ☐

The driver was distracted and the car ran into a ditch. ☐

Playing ball on the green is expressly forbidden. ☐

The train to Leeds has just departed. ☐

want, watch, walk, water, wash, above, love

chins chickens chips

The farmer needed some grain to feed his ___.

licking loaned long

My dog loves barking all day ___.

clod clock clog

I put your hammer on the shelf above the ___.

boy bun bunk

You can sharpen a stick for toasting a ___.

keener keeper killer

He kicked the ball above the goal ___.

chain chicken chair

I saw that loafer sleeping in my ___.

choke clock cake

Could you help me bake a ___?

look lake like

Should we take the foot path down to the ___?

FLUENCY   READING

chart	chair	terse	Hoy	☐ ☆ ★
chard	hash	hoard	lack	☐ ☆ ★
foal	quiz	soar	thug	☐ ☆ ★
quail	gorse	sharp	air	☐ ☆ ★
with	soil	lord	core	☐ ☆ ★
bust	Kay	yank	fort	☐ ☆ ★
and	shack	fist	carve	☐ ☆ ★
leer	held	toil	lamp	☐ ☆ ★
cheep	dunk	verve	tank	☐ ☆ ★
deed	chair	jump	loath	☐ ☆ ★
help	quip	lend	oath	☐ ☆ ★
send	gash	board	land	☐ ☆ ★
main	dent	born	silk	☐ ☆ ★

Mike, the Loan Shark.

Mark watched Hank, the hunch-backed horse, drag himself from the sludge in the yucky pond. Hank was reeking of rotten eggs and sticky weeds were hanging from his neck. Hank kept slipping back as he walked up the bank back to the slushy trail.

Mark said, "You are a right sight, and you are such a smelly horse."

Hank said, "I am just a horse and all horses are slightly smelly. We must walk quickly if we want to find Mike, the loan shark, before dark."

On his way, Hank pointed to all the best sights in the tip. There were junk fridges sunk into patches of green sludge. They saw stacks of rotten spuds and lots of stinking fish.

Hank said, "I like this dump. It's the best junk yard in the land."

Mike, the loan shark, lived in a very big lake with his pal, Patch, the pointless pike. Mike was very rich, and he liked to play with his posh train set. His train could take him to Groan's store, or it could take him to the pub for a drink. Mike was very flash, and he wore lots of bling. He had five studs and a gold chain on his fin.

"How can I help you?" he asked.

Mark said, "I need some cash so I can get a shirt, some shorts and a pair of trainers. I am a boy who is six and I should not have to dress in a ragged shirt with sleeves a yard long, baggy shorts that will not stay up and pink flip-flops. If you can loan me five quid, all will be well."

Mike waited a bit and then he asked "How can you repay me? You are just a small boy. Do you have a job? If you need a job, you should go to see Luke, the Duke of the dump. He can help you get a job."

Then Mike, the loan shark, swam off with his pal Patch, the pointless pike.

Mastery Test

If your pupil does not pass this test they must go back to page 44. This is very important—a child who is struggling will not be learning. Contrary to what you would think, most children would rather go back than carry on getting things wrong. If your pupil needs to go back, use a different coloured pencil for ticking the boxes.

Use the cursor as you would on a Fluency Reading page.

Timed reading: 'Pass' mark is 15 seconds per line.

pitch	remark	rake	hardly	☐
biggest	fight	unless	choke	☐
nuke	joist	bridge	pretend	☐
discuss	trike	chore	match	☐

Reading accuracy: Pass mark is one mistake.

Do not prompt. You may allow your pupil to self correct, but you cannot say anything except "Try again".

You must not distract Luke before lunch. ☐

Mike had a red blotch where the midge bit him. ☐

The farmer dug a ditch to prevent the water
from getting in. ☐

Could you explain why you forgot to switch off
the lights ☐

ir, ur, -ce, -ge

large	lice	charge	cage	bird	☐
Bruce	choice	girl	hurry	church	☐
shirt	price	pence	urge	dance	☐

Some very large lice are sleeping in my bed. ☐

What did they charge you for that bird cage? ☐

I think that Bruce made the right choice. ☐

The girls should hurry up if they are going to church. ☐

You can have that shirt for the price of ten pence! ☐

Joyce	voice	strange	stage	right	☐
twice	change	birch	fence	hurt	☐
Grace	burn	since	Greece	turn	☐
page	face	dirt	nice	birth	☐

Do you think that Joyce has a strange voice? ☐

If you turn right, you will fall off the stage. ☐

We had to change trains twice on the way to Leeds. ☐

Can you see that small bird up in the birch tree? ☐

Grace hurt her leg jumping the fence. ☐

My sunburn hurts since we got back from Greece. ☐

61

DECODING ⚡ POWER ⚡ PAGE

Do not award ticks for a 'good try'—your pupil will pay for it later!

hutch	edge	sigh	twitch	☐
large	girl	nice	burn	☐
resit	beyond	unhappy	extend	☐
mice	cage	turn	bird	☐
take	coke	chuck	bike	☐
firm	pence	fringe	curl	☐
bridge	bright	stitch	budge	☐
richest	lucky	blushes	painful	☐
burst	skirt	place	barge	☐
prepaid	disarm	reload	belay	☐
huge	curve	prince	fir	☐
might	latch	grudge	thigh	☐
hoarded	jointed	queerly	falling	☐
ledge	fright	scotch	sludge	☑

62

Wordbuilder

Remember to practise the flashcards at least once a day!

dress	address	addressed	☑
plain	explain	explained	☐
just	adjust	adjusting	☐
want	wanted	unwanted	☐

Is that letter addressed to me? ☐

Bruce just explained how to make a bridge. ☐

Grace is adjusting the chain on her bike. ☐

You could give your unwanted shirts to Royce. ☐

port	report	reported	☐
act	exact	exactly	☐
mit	admit	admitted	☐
play	replay	replaying	☐
pect	expect	expecting	☐

Joyce has reported her cat missing. ☐

Luke admitted that he broke the glass. ☐

Martha is expecting you back for lunch. ☐

I am fed up with replaying that film. ☐

Your report will be bad if your sums are not exactly right. ☑

want, watch, walk, water, wash, above, love

duck   dog   drink

I want to watch him wash the black ___.

cake   chick   clock

Did he wake up at three o'___?

thighs   blocked   needless

The water in the lake hardly ever gets above my ___.

stake   stink   stop

Put your foot hard on the brake and your car will ___.

song   socks   soap

I wash my feet with ___ and water.

jocks   jokes   jumps

I love the ___ my gran tells.

grass   grip   smoke

If I am feeling better, I will rake the ___.

cat   car   cheer

Put down your ball and help me wash the ___.

FLUENCY READING

rock	cost	reef	kip	□ ☆ ☆
mink	hair	ant	Joan	□ ☆ ☆
barn	pong	nick	worn	□ ☆ ☆
null	weld	fore	sing	□ ☆ ☆
aim	lush	imp	kerf	□ ☆ ☆
quench	yam	risk	peer	□ ☆ ☆
fond	roach	sash	lunch	□ ☆ ☆
term	chill	bun	past	□ ☆ ☆
boar	daft	fay	seek	□ ☆ ☆
went	thong	port	belt	□ ☆ ☆
oat	chip	hang	mush	□ ☆ ☆
oar	ramp	odd	muck	□ ☆ ☆
end	quip	for	tact	□ ☆ ☆

Luke, the Duke of the Dump.

Mike, the loan shark, swam back and said to Mark, "You seem like a nice kid. You can take my train to see Luke, the Duke of the dump. Take your pal, Hank, with you and you can catch the six o'clock train."

Mark thanked Mike. He walked ten paces up the road with Hank, then turned right to get to the railway. They boarded the train and sat in some soft chairs, for they were going first class.

A large man with a badge asked them, "Can I see your passes?"

Hank said, "Mike, the loan shark, said we could catch a lift on his train. You would not want to mess with Mike. We are going to see Luke, the Duke of the dump."

The large man with a badge scratched his shirt, which was full of mice. He said, "Then it must be alright. If Mike is your pal, there will be no charge for this trip. Have a nice day, and do not forget to change trains at the church by the strange bridge."

Hank said to Mark, "This is just grand. It is very nice to sit in a first-class coach. By rights, us horses should go in third-class coaches, for we are dirty, and we pong. But who am I to say 'No' to a soft chair?"

Then the train started with a lurch and they were on the way to see Luke, the Duke of the Dump. The train went faster and faster, and they could see the dump go by in a blur. They saw lots of black smoke from burning boxes. They saw hills of rusty bikes. The large man with a badge served them glasses of cola. It was so nice in Mike's train that they fell asleep. They missed the stop at the church by the strange bridge and the train went speeding on into the night—and Mark still had not had any lunch.

au, aw

| caught | Paul | hawk | lawn | saw | ☐ |
| taught | draw | fawn | thaw | dawn | ☐ |

Paul caught the ball. ☐

I saw a hawk catch some mice on the lawn. ☐

Who taught you how to draw? ☐

At dawn, we saw a deer with her fawn. ☐

Wait for the ice to thaw before you go for a swim. ☐

brawl	fault	paw	because	crawl	☐
launch	prawns	trawl	haul	sprawl	☐
yawn	vault	sauce	jaw	pause	☐

It is not my fault that I got into a brawl! ☐

Joyce likes lots of sauce on her chips. ☐

Our dog could hardly crawl because she hurt her paw. ☐

I like to sprawl across my nice soft bed. ☐

When can we launch the sailing boat? ☐

The trawler caught lots of prawns. ☐

Your car will need a hitch if you want to haul a trailer. ☑

I like to have a good yawn when I first wake up. ☐

DECODING ⚡ POWER ⚡ PAGE

Some of these words are unusual but they are all real words.

slight	witch	dodge	nigh	☐
saw	Paul	yawn	haul	☐
snatch	dredge	flight	hitch	☐
lawn	fraud	draw	cause	☐
bespoke	uncoil	export	prechill	☐
launch	drawn	claw	fault	☐
spice	first	singe	church	☐
flock	tuck	trike	cake	☐
law	pause	thaw	vault	☐
smudge	bight	retch	cadge	☐
maul	flaw	brawn	taut	☐
nurse	plaice	sir	rage	☐
passes	quilting	sister	stressful	☐
sauce	drawl	raw	haunch	☐

Wordbuilder

If your pupil makes a mistake, back up the cursor and sound out the word.

fast	fasten	fastened	unfastened	☐
plore	explore	exploring		☐
sink	sinkable	unsinkable		☐
fright	frighten	frightened		☐

The smart cat unfastened the latch with her paw. ☐

Paul loves to go exploring in strange places. ☐

There is no such thing as an unsinkable ship. ☐

Are you frightened to go into the haunted shack? ☐

block	blocking	unblocking		☐
flat	flatten	flattened		☐
light	relight	relighting		☐
fill	refill	refillable	unrefillable	☐
sweet	sweeten	sweetened	unsweetened	☐

I like my hot drinks unsweetened. ☐

Take the matches for relighting the gas cooker. ☐

Did your dad have a go at unblocking the drains? ☐

My dad gets his beer in unrefillable kegs. ☐

The coins that fell on the rail were flattened by the train. ☐

cook, book, look, foot, good, took, what, when, which

long   lost   load

We should go and look for the ball that we ___.

play   playing   player

What song are the band___?

camp   cook   crack

You will need a ___ book if you are going to bake a cake.

smoke   smock   small

You may get sick if you have a ___.

bricks   blocks   brakes

My bike will not stop if the ___ are no good.

wash   wake   want

When you poke the dog, it will ___ up.

bet   bent   best

Which book do you like ___?

take   tack   tall

My helper loaded up the van with junk to ___ to the dump.

FLUENCY READING

☐ Pass: 10 sec.   ☆ Bonus: 8 sec.   ⚝ Double Bonus: 6 sec.

hark	deer	pink	lax	☐ ☆ ⚝
chick	sung	jail	born	☐ ☆ ⚝
moist	carve	shore	chimp	☐ ☆ ⚝
huff	think	punch	soy	☐ ☆ ⚝
quilt	wimp	teem	fair	☐ ☆ ⚝
bung	bell	tern	serf	☐ ☆ ⚝
joint	yarn	chop	zest	☐ ☆ ⚝
ore	win	ring	load	☐ ☆ ⚝
thank	kiln	gosh	port	☐ ☆ ⚝
gasp	lair	gaff	quest	☐ ☆ ⚝
coy	pick	dump	feel	☐ ☆ ⚝
quill	melt	queer	Max	☐ ☆ ⚝
pelt	quail	perch	song	☐ ☆ ⚝

72

Paul, the Gawky Hawk.

Mark woke up and took a good look at his watch, and he saw that it was ten o'clock. It was a dark night and the train went speeding on. Hank, the hunch-backed horse, was sprawled in his soft chair, snoring in his sleep. Mark gave Hank a poke in the jaw and the horse woke up.

Mark said, "It is dark and my mum will miss me. By now she will have called the cops. What can we do?"

Hank had a good stretch and a good yawn. Then he said, "Why, I cannot say what we should do. Hunch-backed horses are not all that bright at night."

Just then, they saw the large man with a badge. He was bringing more drinks and some cake to keep them awake.

He said, "You have missed your stop. You should have changed trains at the church by the strange bridge. We passed that stop a long way back."

Mark asked, "What can we do? I must call my mum, or she might think I have been flattened by a truck."

The large man with a badge scratched his shirt, which was still full of mice. "I cannot say," he said, "because I am not that smart, but I will call Paul, the gawky hawk, because he is a very, very smart bird."

The large man with a badge called for Paul, the gawky hawk, who came flying into the coach. Paul landed on the back of a chair and dug his claws into the cloth.

"What can I do for you?" he squawked (for he was a hawk). "I am a very, very smart bird, and I can do anything."

Mark asked, "Can you tell my mum that I have come to no harm? I think she likes me a lot."

Paul the gawky hawk stretched his wing and scratched his maw. "Why not? Is there anything more I can do for you?"

Hank, the hunch-backed horse woke up and said, "How can we get back and change trains at the church by the strange bridge? We need to go and see Luke, the Duke of the dump."

Paul plucked a quill from his tail and picked his teeth, (he was lucky to have teeth because hawks do not have teeth).

"Just turn your watch back to seven o'clock. This train stops at the church by the strange bridge at seven." With a smart squawk, Paul went flying off into the next coach.

Word Search

gawky	are
strange	awe
nicely	ice
light	ply
harpy	tree
truce	jaw
rake	luke

s	t	r	a	n	g	e
i	r	a	w	i	a	c
l	u	k	e	c	w	a
i	c	e	i	e	k	u
g	e	a	p	l	y	s
h	a	r	p	y	n	e
t	r	e	e	j	a	w

-tch, -dge, -igh

If your pupil makes a mistake, back up the cursor and sound out the word.

budge	Dutch	smudge	slight	night	☐
flight	lodge	sketch	fudge	fridge	☐
match	fight	watch	cadge	wedge	☐

When the washing-up is done, we can watch the match. ☐

The Dutch boy says he will not budge. ☐

There is a slight smudge on your face. ☐

We took the last flight of the night. ☐

Luke can draw a sketch of the hunting lodge. ☐

Did you put the fudge in the fridge? ☐

patch	stitch	might	nudge	witch	☐
sledge	hitch	light	switch	bright	☐
pitch	stretch	dodge	bridge	sight	☐

Ask Madge to stitch a patch on your shirt. ☐

Give the witch a nudge and she might wake up. ☐

The farmer hitched his horse to the sledge. ☐

Could you switch off the bright lights? ☐

We had to dodge the cars that were crossing the bridge. ☐

They took the player off the football pitch on a stretcher. ☐

DECODING ⚡ POWER ⚡ PAGE

Remember to practise the flashcards at least once a day!

jaunt	sawn	yaw	spawn	☐
Wight	clutch	trudge	blight	☐
forge	slurp	farce	swirl	☐
botch	pledge	high	Dutch	☐
jaw	faun	saucer	gawk	☐
snitch	nigh	drudge	crutch	☐
craw	flaunt	prawn	haunt	☐
sigh	midge	crutch	match	☐
Turk	slice	cringe	smirk	☐
distort	restock	bedeck	unspoilt	☐
patch	thigh	sledge	blotch	☐
trawl	paw	taunt	Maud	☐
cake	fluke	spike	woke	☐
glitch	fight	crotch	wedge	☐

Wordbuilder

Always use the cursor!

turn	return	returned	☐
thank	thankful	thankfully	☐
tend	pretend	pretended	☐
dress	undress	undressing	☐

Paul returned from the pub crawl at ten o'clock. ☐

Thankfully, they have shifted all that sludge for us. ☐

The hawk pretended that it had hurt its claw. ☐

Do not watch when I am undressing. ☐

stack	stacking	restacking	☐
serve	served	reserved	☐
plain	explain	explained	☐
play	display	displayed	☐
miss	dismiss	dismissed	☐

Joyce got a job restacking the shelves at the store. ☐

Have you reserved a place for the match tonight? ☐

Mike just explained how to catch a pike. ☐

We were dismissed when we had done a good job. ☐

My best painting is displayed on the board in the hall.

cook, book, look, foot, good, took, what, when, which

dragged   quake   sadly

Look what the cat ___ in!

lump   lunch   long

When are you going to have ___?

foot   look   good

I put my ___ in my sock

was   wake   watch

When you shake him he will ___ up.

fishing   fixing   falling

I like to watch my dad when he is ___ the car.

bond   boast   boat

Which ___ should we sail on the lake?

fast   fish   Fred

Did Luke choke on that lump of ___?

where   wake   water

My dog shakes off the ___ when he gets wet.

FLUENCY READING

☐ Pass: 10 sec. ☆ Bonus: 8 sec. ★ Double Bonus: 6 sec.

teen	pork	chink	roar	☑ ☆ ★
rig	jilt	void	bunch	☑ ☆ ★
frog	oat	clock	quell	☑ ☆ ★
blot	lung	twill	sheer	☑ ☆ ★
elf	twin	rail	flag	☑ ☆ ★
morn	droll	chunk	slop	☑ ☆ ★
bore	foist	still	hoist	☑ ☆ ★
pram	char	flock	act	☑ ☆ ★
green	fair	bang	snap	☑ ☆ ★
bay	swim	sport	grit	☑ ☆ ★
vest	crab	hoard	prim	☑ ☆ ★
teeth	skid	tuck	chat	☑ ☆ ★
clink	moan	lore	tuft	☑ ☆ ★

Smudge, the Batty Cat.

When Paul, the gawky hawk, had flapped his way into the next coach.

Mark said, "I may as well turn back my watch." But he forgot to take some cake from the large man with the badge, so Hank, the hunch-backed horse, scoffed the lot.

When the hands on Mark's watch were set at seven o'clock, the train stopped at the church by the strange bridge. Mark and Hank stepped off the coach into broad daylight.

"Why, this is all right," said Hank, "Now we can catch the train that will take us to see Luke, the Duke of the dump."

Mark wished he had some lunch. He wished he was with his pal Vern, and he wanted to see Froid, the pet snail. He even wanted a sniff of Bart, the damp dog. But most of all he wanted some shorts, a shirt and some trainers to make him look smart.

Then they met Smudge, the batty cat who wore a flat cap. Smudge said, "I live in the church by the strange bridge, and I catch lots of nice mice and fat rats. Would you like to meet the mice I have caught? They are very nice."

Mark said, "Thank you, but we must be getting on to see Luke, the Duke of the dump. The large man with a badge said that we have to change here."

Smudge asked, "What would you like to change into?"

Mark said, "I would like to change into a nice, new shirt that fits me, some shorts that stay up and some smart trainers."

"You cannot do that," said Smudge, "for this is not a store. Would you like to change into a witch? Witches can cast spells and I should think they have lots of fun."

But Mark did not want to be a witch. "We just want to change trains," he said.

Smudge, the batty cat (who wore a flat cap) said, "Why, you cannot change trains. Even witches cannot change trains into something else."

Mark said, "But we must change trains because we are going to see Luke, the Duke of the dump."

Smudge said, "Then you had best take a boat and go up the creepy creek that runs under the strange bridge. You can take my boat if you wish."

Mastery Test

If your pupil does not pass this test they must go back to page 61. This is very important—a child who is struggling will not be learning. Contrary to what you would think, most children would rather go back than carry on getting things wrong. If your pupil needs to go back, use a different coloured pencil for ticking the boxes.

Use the cursor as you would on a Fluency Reading page.

Timed reading: 'Pass' mark is 15 seconds per line.

charge	patch	disgust	joined	☐
rainy	burn	sketch	recall	☐
express	sharpest	face	judge	☐
bright	undress	predict	dirty	☐

Reading accuracy: Pass mark is one mistake.
Do not prompt. You may allow your pupil to self correct, but you cannot say anything except "Try again".

Joyce had to dodge the cars crossing the bridge. ☐

How much did you charge Bruce for washing his shirt. ☐

Grace had to change her flight for her trip to Greece. ☐

The girls had to hurry to get to church. ☐

Split Digraph

If your pupil makes a mistake, back up the cursor and sound out the word.

time	home	came	same	hope	smile	☐
game	those	name	rope	safe	cope	☐
late	made	ride	spade	lane	prude	☐
trade	pine	Clive	pile	hide	nude	☐

We all came home at the same time. ☐

What is the name of the game? ☐

I hope you can cope with those ropes. ☐

We were late, but we made it home safely. ☐

I will trade my spade for a ride up the lane. ☐

Clive will hide in that pile of pine logs. ☐

June	shine	stale	date	these	ale	☐
pipe	rude	nine	grapes	pale	wipe	☐
dude	ripe	ate	hole	five	use	☐
stole	Pete	fuse	mole	Jane	zone	☐

That dude was very rude to June. ☑

Wipe that pipe until it shines. ☑

The pale ale is a bit stale. ☑

I ate five ripe grapes and nine of these dates. ☐

The mole stole back into its hole. ☑

Did Pete use the right fuse? ☐

84

DECODING ⚡ POWER ⚡ PAGE

Always use the cursor!

sketch	sludge	light	itch	☐
made	hide	home	June	☐
brawl	vaunt	crawl	haul	☐
these	wide	hope	lane	☐
dawn	taut	gaunt	thaw	☐
cute	mole	safe	wipe	☐
light	grudge	notch	Wight	☐
age	lance	curb	twirl	☐
tube	wise	tame	note	☐
fawn	maul	pawn	auk	☐
shine	tale	stone	mule	☐
batch	pledge	might	fetch	☐
failed	gormless	oaken	vainly	☐
cube	bite	lone	tape	☐

Wordbuilder

take   mistake   mistakable   unmistakable   ☐

use   used   unused   ☐

time   timed   mistimed   ☐

sell   selling   reselling   ☐

With your green hair, you are unmistakable.   ☐

Could you return your unused books?   ☐

We crashed because I mistimed that turn.   ☐

Pete made ten quid by reselling that bike.   ☐

rel   relate   related   ☐

ripe   ripen   ripened   unripened   ☐

line   lined   unlined   ☐

port   report   reporter   ☐

quote   quoted   misquoted   ☐

Is Clive related to you or is he just a good mate?   ☐

Dale mistimed the punch line when telling that joke. ☐

That unripened plum will make you ill.   ☐

Jane likes to draw on unlined paper.   ☐

The reporter misquoted the speech.   ☐

teach, real, eat, please, year, leave, reach, meat, friend

hitch   hall   hedge

Please leave your coats in the___.

toads   slime   meat

Last year, Clive and Jane gave up eating ___.

meat   meet   cook

Pete is really keen to ___ your friends.

reach   real   eat

Can you ___ the book on the top shelf.

desk   tent   lake

Could my friends go swimming in your ___?

took   torch   toiled

Did you see which book Jean ___?

song   sang   sing

When will you teach me how to ___?

porch   poke   pork

We could roast some ___ to eat.

FLUENCY READING

grab	hush	flit	perch	☐ ☆ ★
orb	bluff	play	pair	☐ ☆ ★
silk	drill	chard	fled	☐ ☆ ★
maths	tor	grass	gait	☐ ☆ ★
oar	blob	shark	ask	☐ ☆ ★
class	neck	quick	plan	☐ ☆ ★
coil	seer	hump	crack	☐ ☆ ★
woad	chuck	grip	torch	☐ ☆ ★
tart	pang	more	loach	☐ ☆ ★
drip	joint	verse	flop	☐ ☆ ★
corm	josh	mend	beer	☐ ☆ ★
hay	glass	stay	kith	☐ ☆ ★
clam	cheep	yard	nest	☐ ☆ ★

Floyd, the Faultless Fish.

Smudge, the batty cat—who wore a flat cap—took Mark and Hank to the creepy creek, where his boat was parked.

"This is a very safe boat," he said, "It is made of the finest pine and it is nine yards long and five feet wide."

"It is just the right size for a hunch-backed horse." Hank said, "How can we find the way to see Luke, the Duke of the dump?"

Smudge said, "You must meet my mate. His name is Floyd, the faultless fish. He is a good sole and he is very wise. He will take you where you want to go."

Then Smudge spotted some cute mice and he went back in the cat-flap into the church by the strange bridge. Hank and Mark got into Smudge's boat and they shook hands with Floyd, the faultless fish. Or they had to pretend to shake hands, because fish do not have hands.

"We must go quickly if we want to catch the tide," said Floyd.

Mark cast off the ropes, and Smudge's boat sailed away. The tide in the creepy creek ran quite fast and they had to watch out for barges and whales. Mark had to steer because horses cannot steer boats. They stopped for a while when Floyd met a skate who was his best mate. Hank sat on the oars and watched the water slide by.

"This is the life," he said, "I should have been a sailor."

Floyd, the faultless fish, stopped again and scratched his nose.

"Eeny, meeny, miny, mo, which way should I go?" he asked, flapping his fin to right and left.

"What a shame," he said, "I think we are lost. There are too many creeks in this place and they all look the same." Just then Floyd spotted a snack bar on the side of the creek.

"We must go to that snack bar and find out where we are," he said,pointing to a large shack on the bank

Mark and Hank got out of the boat and went up the slope to the snack bar.

"I must have a drink," said Hank, "and I must get one for Floyd. I bet he drinks like a fish."

But Mark did not want a drink. "What have you got for lunch?" he asked the girl in the snack bar.

"It is too late for a plate of cooked food," she said, "But you can have a bag of hedgehog crisps. They are made from fresh road-kill, and they are very nice."

....

Mastery Test

If your pupil who does not pass this test they must go back to page 84. This is very important—a child who is struggling will not be learning. Contrary to what you would think, most children would rather go back than carry on getting things wrong. If your pupil needs to go back, use a different coloured pencil for ticking the boxes.

Use the cursor as you would on a Fluency Reading page.

Timed reading: 'Pass' mark is 15 seconds per line.

rude	lawn	expand	trawler	☐
matches	trade	sauce	prefix	☐
drawing	lighter	hope	fault	☐
hawk	crawled	misjudge	wipe	☐

Reading accuracy: Pass mark is one mistake.
Do not prompt. You may allow your pupil to self correct, but you cannot say anything except "Try again".

Paul hitched up the trailer to haul the boat to the water. ☐

Clive was late but he still got home safely. ☐

Jane got up at dawn and saw a hawk on the lawn. ☐

Pete and June are going to pick grapes in France. ☐

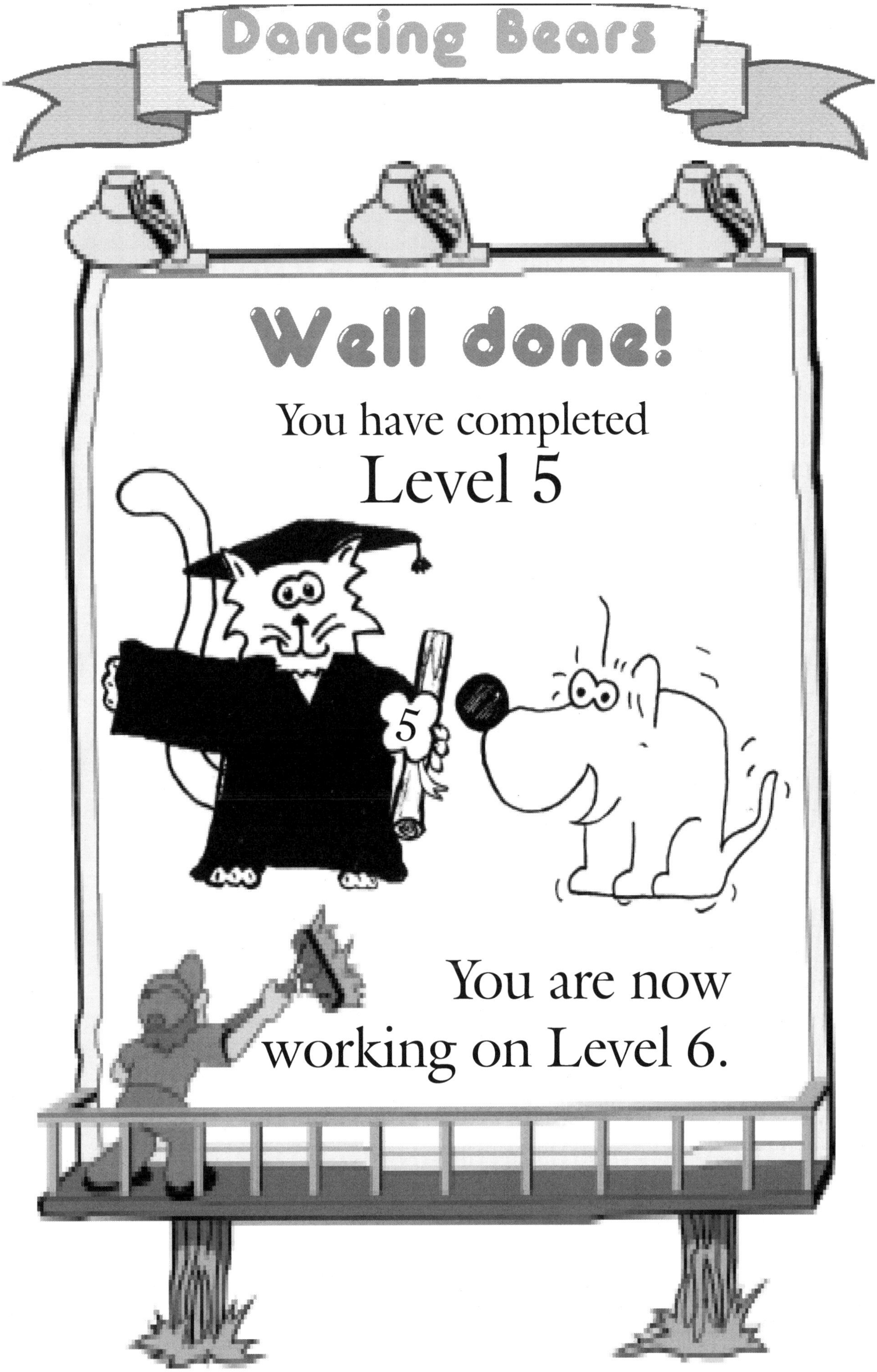
Dancing Bears
Well done!
You have completed
Level 5
5
You are now
working on Level 6.

ir, ur, -ce, -ge

Do not award ticks for a 'good try'—your pupil will pay for it later!

prince	dance	chirp	bird	race	☐
office	nice	sage	mince	curly	☐
Turk	plunge	urge	squirt	slurp	☐

The prince asked the fair maiden to go to the dance. ☐

Birds like to chirp in the morning. ☐

I will race you back to the office. ☐

Mince cooked with sage is very nice. ☐

Do Turks have curly hair? ☐

Any time you get the urge, just plunge into the lake. ☐

purse	birth	plaice	sauce	surf	☐
chance	wage	nurse	spruce	huge	☐
dirty	barge	bilge	range	firm	☐

My sister gave Marge a purse for her birthday. ☐

Do you like sauce with your plaice and chips? ☐

This is your last chance to ride a surfboard. ☐

Do nurses get paid a good wage? ☐

We sat next to the huge spruce tree. ☐

The bilges of a barge are full of dirty water. ☐

Remember to practise the flashcards at least once a day!

date	life	hole	fuse	☐
plunge	murk	chance	birth	☐
witch	dodge	right	badge	☐
urn	sage	flirt	face	☐
jaw	awl	gauze	sauce	☐
frailest	reborn	porky	belong	☐
same	side	bone	theme	☐
daub	law	cause	Paul	☐
hinge	lurk	race	shirt	☐
switch	fudge	night	hedge	☐
irk	dice	burp	bilge	☐
Pete	rise	pale	prune	☐
paw	fraud	bawl	taunt	☐
purse	wage	voice	dirt	☐

Wordbuilder

Always use the cursor!

pute	dispute	disputed	undisputed	☐
want	wanted	unwanted		☐
float	floated	refloated		☐
charge	charged	recharged		☐

My darts team is the undisputed winner of the match.   ☐

Please leave all your unwanted books here.   ☐

After my boat sank, the divers refloated it.   ☐

Dad has just recharged his cordless drill.   ☐

friend	friendly	unfriendly	☐
place	replace	replacement	☐
turn	return	returning	☐
slice	sliced	unsliced	☐
place	placed	misplaced	☐

I have not lost my glasses, I have just misplaced them.   ☐

Do you think that dog is unfriendly?   ☐

Paul wants me to get an unsliced loaf at the shop.   ☐

Joyce and Maud will be returning at nine o'clock.   ☐

If that shirt is no good, we will give you a replacement.   ☐

teach, real, eat, please, year, leave, reach, meat, friend

glass   class   mass

When can we leave this ___?

road   roach   roast

If you honk your horn, he will get off the ___.

sings   six   sinks

Next year I will be ___.

good   got   stake

My teacher is very ___ to me.

shall   shell   shelf

Can you reach the book on the top___?

ask   eat   end

I did not mean to ___ all the meat.

like   leave   last

Please Miss, may I ___ my seat?

lung   link   long

My dog is getting fatter now that he eats all day ___.

FLUENCY READING

nest	Claire	loin	swig	☐ ☆ ★
laid	peck	skill	quit	☐ ☆ ★
beef	film	hoard	Cain	☐ ☆ ★
king	norm	twig	Ark	☐ ☆ ★
elm	verse	flap	sheer	☐ ☆ ★
foil	aft	chit	fret	☐ ☆ ★
meek	dung	sack	drop	☐ ☆ ★
core	goad	bank	quilt	☐ ☆ ★
snip	short	mist	berth	☐ ☆ ★
bran	bairn	boy	champ	☐ ☆ ★
inch	plum	tosh	quench	☐ ☆ ★
luck	stab	boar	ail	☐ ☆ ★
shelf	sort	swill	peep	☐ ☆ ★

Dawn's Snack Bar.

Hank, the hunch-backed horse, took a full pail of fizzy drink and went off to slurp it down with Floyd, the faultless fish.

The girl in the snack bar said to Mark, "You should try hedgehog crisps, because they are made from fresh road-kill. They are very nice when you wash them down with a glass of dirty ditch water."

Mark said, "Thank you, but I don't want hedgehog crisps. Hedgehogs have sharp quills, and one might get stuck in my throat."

The girl in the snack bar wiped down the counter with a grubby rag. She said, "My name is Dawn. They call me Dawn because I can talk until dawn, or until you start to yawn, whichever comes first. What do they call you? Dirty Shirt?"

Mark said, "I cannot help being dirty and the shirt is not mine. If I ever get to meet Luke, the Duke of the dump, then I will get a job. Then I can get a loan from Mike, the loan shark, and then I can get a pair of shorts and a shirt from Groan, the croaking toad. Then you will see that I can be smart."

Dawn said, "You are very dirty. When you live in a dump, shirts and shorts get dirty very quickly. You will never get a job looking like that. Come over here and take this robe."

So Mark went to step behind the counter of the snack bar, but just then he fell right over his big pink flip flops and went down with a thud.

"Ha ha... Maybe you need some trainers too," said Dawn. "Now give that shirt to me and I will wash it for you. Put on this green bathrobe and I will rinse the grime and sludge from your shirt. At the same time, we might as well wash those big, baggy shorts."

Just then, Hank the hunch-backed horse, came back and said, "I must help Floyd the faultless fish. A man just came in and asked for fish and chips. Floyd is legless, for he is a fish. I must help him get away."

Mark said, "I cannot go because this bathrobe belongs to Dawn and she is washing my shirt and shorts. What can we do?"

Split digraph

If your pupil makes a mistake, back up the cursor and sound out the word.

Clive	jade	wrote	note	bike	tube	☐
Jane	mine	robe	white	stone	prune	☐
those	bite	make	fine	gate	pine	☐

Jade wrote a note to Clive. ☐

Do not bite hard on those prunes—they have stones. ☐

I will make the gate with the finest pine. ☐

Jane had to patch the tube on her bike. ☐

The white bath robe is mine. ☐

skate	ice	rode	hate	quite	mate	☐
Pete	home	late	rule	wife	Clive	☐
make	bone	shame	alone	tales	Jane	☐
sale	crate	these	wine	style	froze	☐

Pete rode home quite late last night. ☐

Clive's wife makes all the rules at home. ☐

My mate hates to skate on thin ice. ☐

Leave the dog alone with his bone. ☐

It's a shame that Jane is telling tales. ☐

These crates of wine are on sale. ☐

DECODING ⚡ POWER ⚡ PAGE

Some of these words are unusual but they are all real words.

pace	birch	lunge	furl	☐
late	mile	rule	rode	☐
fault	trawl	Maud	raw	☐
quote	pipe	line	sale	☐
notch	sight	clutch	cadge	☐
tune	quite	name	scope	☐
fleece	spurt	ice	chirp	☐
saw	faun	drawn	vaunt	☐
time	use	flame	cope	☐
unaided	exactly	precast	disbanding	☐
ate	Clive	pole	rude	☐
verge	lurch	force	quirk	☐
gauze	flaw	pawn	haunt	☐
hate	dude	robe	swipe	☐

Wordbuilder

Do not award ticks for a 'good try'—your pupil will pay for it later!

firm	confirm	confirmed	unconfirmed	☐
play	played	misplayed		☐
part	depart	departing		☐
light	delight	delighted		☐
port	report	reports		☐

We have unconfirmed reports of a space-ship landing. ☐

We lost because the goalkeeper misplayed the ball. ☐

I will be delighted to see my friends again. ☐

The train to Dover will be departing at nine o'clock. ☐

wise	unwise	unwisely	☐
change	changed	unchanged	☐
give	forgive	forgiven	☐
fess	confess	confessed	☐
skill	skilful	skilfully	☐

Small boys and girls sometimes act unwisely. ☐

The score is still unchanged. ☐

Jane plays the game very skilfully. ☐

You will be forgiven if you have confessed your crime. ☐

teach, real, eat, please, year, leave, reach, meat, friend

wake   will   want

Please walk softly or you will ___ my mum.

rich   real   ring

His hair is not ___ , he has a wig!

cut   cult   cost

Please put that sharp chopper away, you might ___ your hand.

been   beet   beer

Did you see where he put his glass of ___?

return   retake   reach

My friend is waiting for me to ___ his bike.

join   joist   joint

When will we be eating that ___ of beef?

lake   late   lay

We can go by train if we are not ___.

yours   years   yeast

My dad has been a joiner for ten ___.

FLUENCY READING

loft	shack	brass	pair	☐ ☆ ★
tar	rung	chug	glad	☐ ☆ ★
parse	junk	perch	grim	☐ ☆ ★
shore	baize	pond	quench	☐ ☆ ★
brim	shed	kelp	Seth	☐ ☆ ★
spot	deer	tee	mint	☐ ☆ ★
morse	drop	geese	ink	☐ ☆ ★
pick	swam	oar	noise	☐ ☆ ★
spot	tall	bunk	hotly	☐ ☆ ★
coarse	matted	stay	breech	☐ ☆ ★
runner	landed	served	handed	☐ ☆ ★
sleet	ball	plum	running	☐ ☆ ★
end	wishing	steer	quickly	☐ ☆ ★

Maud, the Maudlin Trawler-Woman.

Hank, the hunch-backed horse, launched the boat that belonged to Smudge, the batty cat with the flat cap. He had to save Floyd, the faultless fish, from a grim fate. Mark waved as they sailed away, and then he went back to Dawn's snack bar and sat next to the coal burning in the grate. Dawn was still washing his shirts and shorts. He really wanted something to eat—anything but hedgehog crisps. Or fish and chips.

Dawn came back and said "Your shirt and shorts are clean now, when they are dry you might get a job. I will talk with Maud, the maudlin trawler woman. She might give you a job trawling for small prawns. But we will need to find you some boots first."

Dawn hung Mark's shirt and shorts to dry by the flames and went off to find Maud, the maudlin trawler woman. After a while, she came back with a pair of dusty boots and a big woman with a wooden nose.

"Here, these boots were mine when I was small. I think they will fit you." she said, "And this is Maud, the maudlin trawler woman."

"Yes, I am Maud," said the woman with the wooden nose. "I may cry a lot, but I catch the best small prawns in this dump. If you want a job on my boat, pull on those boots, I do not give jobs to small boys in big, pink flip-flops."

Dawn said, "I will get you a belt for those big shorts, so you won't end up crawling about."

Mark said, "I will do my best, but I might cry a lot too, because I do still need some lunch."

Dawn yawned as she gave Maud a big mug of tea. She winked at Mark and said, "You might not be very smart, but you look a lot better than you did when you came in here. I bet you will catch lots of prawns, but you will still cry a lot."

Then Maud, the maudlin trawler woman, took a drink from her big mug and took Mark down to her trawler.

Mastery Test

If your pupil does not pass this test they must go back to page 95. This is very important—a child who is struggling will not be learning. Contrary to what you would think, most children would rather go back than carry on getting things wrong. If your pupil needs to go back, use a different coloured pencil for ticking the boxes.

Use the cursor as you would on a Fluency Reading page.

Timed reading: 'Pass' mark is 15 seconds per line.

gate	shirt	thaw	explain	☐
dislike	froze	large	gaunt	☐
yawn	slightly	quite	mice	☐
curly	brawl	pitcher	rule	☐

Reading accuracy: Pass mark is one mistake.
Do not prompt. You may allow your pupil to self correct, but you cannot say anything except "Try again".

Maud rode her bike to the haunted shack. ☐

The nurses walked past the huge plane tree. ☐

Jane stopped to patch the inner tube on her bike. ☐

Pete's wife made a nice cake with ripe prunes. ☐

au, aw

If your pupil makes a mistake, back up the cursor and sound out the word.

Maud	drawn	because	haunt	brawn	☐
hawk	claw	dawn	crawl	pause	☐
sawn	fraud	daub	maul	sprawl	☐

Maud took a ride in a horse-drawn cart. ☐

No one will go in those woods because they are haunted. ☐

This job takes brains, not brawn. ☐

Hawks have very sharp claws. ☐

Dawn had to crawl under the fence. ☐

Shall we pause for a cup of tea? ☐

Paul	vault	Saul	caught	prawn	☐
taught	brawl	jaw	yawn	Paul	☐
dawn	gaunt	drawn	jaunt	sauce	☐

Paul keeps his cash safe in a bank vault. ☐

Maud caught her sleeve on a rose bush. ☐

Who taught you how to catch prawns? ☐

Roy broke his jaw in a brawl. ☐

Paul woke up at dawn and had a good yawn. ☐

Saul looked gaunt and drawn after being so ill. ☐

110

DECODING ⚡ POWER ⚡ PAGE

Do not award ticks for a 'good try'—your pupil will pay for it later!

mate	pine	cute	zone	☐
drawl	pause	claw	gaunt	☐
change	bird	lace	hurt	☐
draw	haunt	Gaul	prawn	☐
edge	bight	catch	smudge	☐
sawn	craw	daub	sauce	☐
retrain	because	unhinge	exerting	☐
slide	gale	Eve	those	☐
caught	crawl	Maud	yawn	☐
mince	flange	burnt	sir	☐
dawn	haunch	gawk	taught	☐
ride	stale	trim	drove	☐
prejudge	distance	switches	burning	☐
lawn	saucer	faun	brawn	☐

Wordbuilder

daunt	daunted	undaunted	☐
hope	hopeless	hopelessly	☐
pect	expect	expected	unexpected ☐
mark	remark	remarkable	☐
dress	address	addressed	☐

The ship sailed on, undaunted by the storm. ☐

We got hopelessly lost when Paul mislaid the map. ☐

Maud's return last night was unexpected. ☐

Floyd scored a remarkable goal in the match today. ☐

That letter is addressed to Dawn. ☐

ply	apply	applying	☐
watch	watchable	unwatchable	☐
stand	understand	understanding	☐
fish	fisher	fisherman	☐

Spike is applying for a job at the chip shop. ☐

That film is so bad that it is unwatchable. ☐

I like my teacher because she is very understanding. ☐

The fisherman caught five roach, a perch and a pike. ☐

teach, real, eat, please, year, leave, reach, meat, friend

Spain   sport   spoil

I really want to go flying to ___.

end   eat   eke

Please leave your seat when the play comes to an ___.

brake   bank   bake

Will your friend help you ___ that cake?

hail   hair   have

Why is your mum cutting your ___?

yard   yank   year

Can we all play football in that ___?

leave   like   last

Why did all of the teachers ___ us here?

cask   cake   cart

My mum let me have a huge slice of ___.

freeze   friend   forge

I found out about this place from my best ___.

□ Pass: 10 sec. ☆ Bonus: 8 sec. ★ Double Bonus: 6 sec.

float	hall	quest	taller	□ ☆ ★
filth	partly	crash	pinned	□ ☆ ★
drab	fitted	fang	fatter	□ ☆ ★
flair	fall	snail	hitting	□ ☆ ★
horn	flatly	snack	small	□ ☆ ★
scar	asking	grill	cutter	□ ☆ ★
jolt	helped	score	nipper	□ ☆ ★
spoil	lastly	scorch	calling	□ ☆ ★
Forth	running	keel	zipper	□ ☆ ★
costly	rotten	handful	stoat	□ ☆ ★
horses	helper	brash	sunken	□ ☆ ★
score	gleeful	quitting	clash	□ ☆ ★
bosses	tapped	tallest	flair	□ ☆ ★

Mark's Dream.

Mark went back down to the creek with Maud, the maudlin trawler woman. Hank, the hunch-backed horse, was not there, and the boat that belonged to Smudge, the batty cat in a flat cap, was gone. Floyd, the faultless fish, was nowhere to be seen and Mark hoped he was not sitting on a plate of chips. Mark felt very sleepy when he boarded Maud's trawler. He fell asleep on a pile of ropes right away.

Mark had some strange dreams. First, Bart, the junk-yard dog, took a loaf and some milk to his mum.

His mum seemed to think that Bart was her son and she said, "Thank you, Mark. You are a good dog, but you took ever such a long time."

Mark was cross because his mum would not look at him and she stroked Bart's damp fur. Then Froid, the pet snail, came in and he was huge. His shell was painted with green letters that said, "For Sale". Vern was with him, but he was very small, and he was sitting in Froid's chair.

Vern said, "You must go to see Groan, the croaking toad. He wants to sell you a shirt and shorts and trainers that fit. He says that he will sell them very cheaply and then you will be the smartest boy again.

Next, Groyne, the grey-green goat, who wore his hair in a quiff, turned up and said, "Herb, the sharp shark, is waiting for you with his bus pass. He will take you to see Jake, the fake snake. Have a chomp on this lovely tin foil."

Mark went down the road and got on the bus. The driver was Mike, the loan shark, who sat next to his friend Patch, the pointless pike. Jake, the fake snake, had become a real snake but he was still missing one of his trainers.

The large man with a badge walked in and said, "This bus will not start. You will have to push it all the way to the tip."

So Mark left his seat and got behind the bus. He pushed it as hard as he could, but it would not budge. His feet were sinking into the moist muck, as he sank down to his thighs until his legs were stuck.

Then Paul, the gawky hawk, landed on his back and squawked, "Push harder! Push harder!"

Mark yelled, "Please help me!"

Then he woke up and saw Maud, the maudlin trawler-woman, standing next to him. She said, "You just missed lunch because you were sleeping, but now you can go down and help wash the dirty dishes."

Split Digraph

Always use the cursor!

bride	white	Jade	skate	blade	close	☐
twine	gate	scone	stale	trade	game	☐
style	robe	cute	late	side	shape	☐

The bride was dressed in white. ☐

Jade should sharpen the blades of her skates. ☐

I will trade my scone for your stale cakes. ☐

Those cute robes are all in the latest style. ☐

Our side must get into shape for the next game. ☐

Do not forget to close the gate and fasten in with twine. ☐

pipes	froze	broke	quite	blame	crime	☐
shame	Pete	ate	cube	flame	close	☐
wise	nine	rise	slope	ice	slide	☐

Those pipes just froze because our heater broke down. ☐

I am not quite sure who to blame for the crime. ☐

It is a shame that Pete ate all the sugar cubes. ☐

Are you sure it is wise to sit so close to the flames? ☐

The sun will rise at nine this morning. ☐

You cannot slide down the slope if there is no ice on it. ☐

DECODING ⚡ POWER ⚡ PAGE

Remember to practise the flashcards at least once a day!

launch	fawn	spawn	yaw	☐
nude	stem	stole	dive	☐
Bruce	surf	merge	quirt	☐
shape	crime	rope	shun	☐
Dutch	trudge	slight	botch	☐
flit	crude	gripe	shame	☐
boarder	tuneful	aired	charmless	☐
midge	blight	switch	budge	☐
Jade	ripe	shed	game	☐
bright	hutch	wedge	ketch	☐
stab	dime	mine	cone	☐
hawk	daub	paw	yawn	☐
reserve	patches	bewitch	flirting	☐
Crete	shade	mine	slope	☐

Wordbuilder

If your pupil makes a mistake, back up the cursor and sound out the word.

play	replay	replayed	☐
treme	extreme	extremely	☐
force	enforce	enforcement	☐
card	discard	discarded	☐

How many times have they replayed that tune? ☐

Gail's grades were extremely bad. ☐

Law enforcement is a cop's main job. ☐

We had to pick up all the discarded cans. ☐

part	depart	department	☐
help	helpless	helplessly	☐
plain	explain	explained	☐
ploy	employ	employed	unemployed ☐
use	useless		☐

My mum likes to go shopping in big department stores. ☐

Paul looked on helplessly as his toy boat sank. ☐

Our teacher has explained that twice so far. ☐

Jake got a job after he had been unemployed for a year. ☐

It is useless trying to explain that to my sister. ☐

☁ ....

out, found, our, loud, house, about, sure, sugar

bank born book

Will you turn the page in our ___?

slipper sleeve sleep

My shirt has got some dirt on the ___.

large purge slur

Our house is not very ___.

cake curd cage

Did you let the bird out of its ___?

loud launch sugar

Dad went mad when he found out about our ___ speakers.

curb slurp girl

I am sure your friend is a very nice ___.

barn burn bun

When you are cooking, you must stir the pot or it will ___.

cake curl curve

You will need lots of sugar to bake a ___.

FLUENCY READING

☐ Pass: 10 sec. ☆ Bonus: 8 sec. ★ Double Bonus: 6 sec.

harmless	hoist	playful	rubbed	☐ ☆ ★
steep	hottest	queer	sharpen	☐ ☆ ★
boxer	creel	fattest	landing	☐ ☆ ★
foxes	adore	fatten	quaint	☐ ☆ ★
smallest	badly	float	musty	☐ ☆ ★
hair	feckless	sorted	broth	☐ ☆ ★
helpful	harder	happy	sneer	☐ ☆ ★
dotty	stern	spotless	falling	☐ ☆ ★
scar	glasses	oar	sticky	☐ ☆ ★
deftly	slain	thicken	witless	☐ ☆ ★
like	gall	back	board	☐ ☆ ★
yuck	fitful	brim	Peke	☐ ☆ ★
hardly	hake	mucky	faint	☐ ☆ ★

Nate, the First Mate.

Maud, the maudlin trawler-woman, said to Mark, "You must go below and help wash the dishes. Just dive down that hatch and you will find the mess decks. That is where the dirty dishes are."

Mark ran down the deck and went below, but he could not find the mess decks.

Then he bumped into a large, smelly dog who barked, "Watch where you are going little boy. I am Nate, the first mate, and I am a sea dog from way back. When Maud is sleeping, I take charge of this trawler." With that, Nate took a puff on his pipe, and a huge cloud of smoke came out of his ears.

Mark said, "Please Sir, I must find the mess decks. Maud said that I should help wash the dirty dishes, but you should not smoke that pipe because it is bad for you."

Nate, the first mate said, "Why, sea dogs must smoke pipes. It is in the rule book. Here, come and look and you will see that I am right."

Nate led Mark to the deck house, and then up to the bridge. The bridge is where they steer a ship, and on the bridge of the trawler Mark saw that they were out to sea. He could not see the dump anywhere—there was water as far as he could see.

Nate, the first mate, got out the rule book and Mark saw that he was right: sea dogs must smoke pipes.

Then Nate said, "I have been a sea dog all my life. Ever since I was a pup, I have sailed the seven seas. I have seen many strange sights and I have seen lamp posts in many strange lands. I have done so many things that are bad for dogs that smoking a pipe hardly matters."

Mark asked, "Please sir, do you think I could have some lunch?"

Nate said, "Why, yes you can. You can have what is left in this can of dog food."

Mark looked at the can of dog food and he felt sick. It was full of slime and rotten meat. He said, "Please sir, can you tell me how to get to the mess decks? Maud will be very cross if I do not help wash the dirty dishes."

 ....

Mastery Test

If your pupil does not pass this test they must go back to page 110. This is very important—a child who is struggling will not be learning. Contrary to what you would think, most children would rather go back than carry on getting things wrong. If your pupil needs to go back, use a different coloured pencil for ticking the boxes.

Use the cursor as you would on a Fluency Reading page.

Timed reading: 'Pass' mark is 15 seconds per line.

sprawl	twine	burning	between	☐
tallest	sawn	slope	switches	☐
handfull	bosses	taught	cute	☐
bride	cutter	sunken	fraud	☐

Reading accuracy: Pass mark is one mistake.
Do not prompt. You may allow your pupil to self correct, but you cannot say anything except "Try again".

Our pipes were frozen when the heater was broken. ☐

June and Clive had to crawl under the fence. ☐

Maud and Paul caught nine large prawns. ☐

Pete and Jade are getting into shape for the big game. ☐

ue, ew

If your pupil makes a mistake, back up the cursor and sound out the word.

Sue	knew	cruel	crew	flew	clue	☐
new	blue	Kew	few	glue	threw	☐
stew	glue	screw	fuel	yew	value	☐

Sue knew that she was being cruel. ☐

The crew flew the new plane over Kew. ☐

Paul drew a few lines in blue paint. ☐

Joyce threw the rotten stew in the bin. ☐

Drew fixed the board with glue and screws. ☐

You can burn those yew logs—they are very good fuel. ☐

true	grew	pew	blue	brew	flue	☐
argue	knew	sue	newt	due	chew	☐
shrew	hue	dew	clue	skew	duel	☐

Is it true that Pete grew five inches last year? ☐

Some blue smoke went up the flue. ☐

Sit in that pew while I brew some tea. ☐

I think he knew when Sue was due back. ☐

A newt cannot chew because it has no teeth. ☐

Never argue with your teacher—it will get you disliked! ☐

Do not award ticks for a 'good try'—your pupil will pay for it later!

pope	trade	five	came	☐
blue	few	yew	stew	☐
auburn	awful	saunter	shawl	☐
Kew	clue	new	Sue	☐
page	skirmish	lice	turf	☐
drew	flew	brew	rue	☐
grip	slime	Luke	ode	☐
kitchen	lodge	fright	scotch	☐
mew	true	newt	glue	☐
launder	tawny	applaud	drawn	☐
fuel	skew	hue	grew	☐
plate	flit	wife	rule	☐
unloader	explode	disgrace	predate	☐
due	chew	pew	flue	☐

Wordbuilder

Always use the cursor!

harm	harmless	harmlessly	☐
fright	frighten	frightening	☐
grace	disgrace	disgraceful	☐
tain	contain	container	☐

The bomb dropped harmlessly into the sea. ☐

Sue won't watch that film because it is too frightening. ☐

Our dog did something disgraceful on the carpet. ☐

You should keep those shells in a steel container. ☐

norm	normal	normally	☐
agree	disagree	disagreement	☐
joy	enjoy	enjoyable	☐
fess	confess	confessed	☐
heat	reheat	reheated	☐

Jane normally gets out of bed at six o'clock. ☐

Floyd had a disagreement with his teacher. ☐

Joyce had a most enjoyable time at the fair. ☐

Paul confessed that he swiped my lighter. ☐

Dawn has just reheated the stew for lunch. ☐

| out, | found, | our, | loud, | house, | about, | sure, | sugar |

weed   weep   week

Are you sure you saw him twice last ___?

burr   blurt   house

Have you got any space left at your ___?

flirt   feed   firm

Our cat will purr out loud if you___ her.

water   merger   furl

The men digging up the road found the burst ___ main.

fudge   fringe   forge

Do you know how to make sugar into __?

church   spice   chips

How much do they charge for a large bag of ___?

net   not   now

Do you know how to surf the ___?

spurn   sponge   spurge

I like to wash my neck with a large ___.

FLUENCY READING

loke	fallen	truck	telling	☐ ☆ ★
hike	queer	stoke	happen	☐ ☆ ★
skip	Jack	stall	nick	☐ ☆ ★
wilful	spoilt	Jake	catty	☐ ☆ ★
duke	flatter	mended	woke	☐ ☆ ★
stair	bike	thinnest	flip	☐ ☆ ★
brick	bloater	luck	backless	☐ ☆ ★
twerp	spike	fastest	hick	☐ ☆ ★
needed	neck	store	kick	☐ ☆ ★
sweeten	band	poke	sweeper	☐ ☆ ★
muck	classes	twain	quack	☐ ☆ ★
smelly	fluke	fairly	track	☐ ☆ ★
cheer	make	chinless	lend	☐ ☆ ★

133

Sue, the Gruesome Stoker.

Nate, the first mate, puffed on his pipe and said, "If Maud wants you to wash the dirty dishes, you had better go and do just that. Nobody messes with Maudlin Maud, not when she has been crying into her tea."

So Mark came down from the bridge, and he kept going down hatches. He found himself down in the bilges of the trawler. It was very hot below because there was black coal burning in the boilers.

Then a loud voice said, "Who are you? My name is Sue. I am Sue, the gruesome stoker. I have a steel ring in my nose, and a blue tattoo on my arm. This is a hard crew, and I am the hardest of the lot. We do not need little boys on this trawler."

"My name is Mark, and I may be a little boy, but I will try to be hard like you." said Mark, "I have good, hard boots now not soft, pink flip flops that trip me up, but my feet hurt and I am very hungry. Maud said that I should wash the dirty dishes, but I cannot find the mess decks. What should I do?"

Sue, the gruesome stoker, said, "Why, you can help me stoke the boilers. If there is no steam in the boilers, the screw will not turn, and then this trawler will not trawl. Pick up that shovel and help me sling coal on the flames."

So Mark picked up the shovel and it was as big as he was, for he was just a small boy. He could not sling coal as well as Sue, the gruesome stoker. She had big beefy arms and she was very strong. She smelled a bit strong, too. The smoke from the burning coal got up Mark's nose and made him sneeze. He was not sure that he liked his new job. Besides, his shirt and shorts were getting dirty again and his dusty boots did not fit well and were hurting his feet.

Then Sue said, "That is just fine for now. The boiler is hot and full of steam. Now we can stop and brew a nice cup of tea."

Mark asked, "Why do they call you the gruesome stoker?"

Sue said, "Well when I was a girl, I was very tall. When my Dad got home from trawling, he would say, "Why Sue, I think you grew some more. You must be six feet tall!"

The tea was so strong that Mark had to put six lumps of sugar in it. It was so strong that Mark had to chew on it. When Sue was not looking, he tipped it down his boots. The tea was so hot that he started hopping up and down.

Sue roared with mirth, "I have never seen such a funny boy," she said. "I think I will keep you here. You are fun to watch."

 ....

If your pupil makes a mistake, back up the cursor and sound out the word.

three	stray	shrub	stroll	street	☐
shrimp	squid	thrash	splash	scream	☐
throat	spring	sprout	sprawl	threw	☐

I can see three stray dogs in the shrubs. ☐

Let's take a stroll down the street. ☐

The fisherman caught some shrimp and a squid. ☐

Please do not thrash and splash in the bath. ☐

You can't scream if you have a sore throat. ☐

In the spring, all the seeds will sprout. ☐

scruff	straw	stress	strain	spruce	☐
string	screw	squeak	shrunk	squall	☐
scrap	squall	thrift	splice	scrape	☐

Our scruffy dog sleeps on a pile of straw. ☐

I can't stand all this stress and strain. ☐

Why is my string hanging from the spruce tree? ☐

Put some oil on the screw and it will not squeak. ☐

My jumper shrunk when I got caught in the rain squall. ☐

Our chickens squawk when we feed them the scraps. ☐

DECODING ⚡ POWER ⚡ PAGE

Some of these words are unusual but they are all real words.

hew	argue	cue	slew	☐
street	throne	shrub	thrill	☐
scrape	grill	strive	grate	☐
split	screed	strip	scrimp	☐
scrawl	straw	paunch	August	☐
stretch	scram	throb	spruce	☐
gruel	Jew	trews	value	☐
churn	stage	squirt	quince	☐
thrash	squeeze	strut	splint	☐
sprite	throve	shrine	astute	☐
squint	three	shred	thrip	☐
skewer	spew	duel	blue	☐
ketch	splodge	tight	scratch	☐
shrimp	spring	splatter	scruffy	☐

Wordbuilder

Always use the cursor!

cord	record	recorder			☐
agree	agreeable	disagreeable			☐
zip	unzip	unzipped			☐
vent	event	eventful	eventfully	uneventfully	☐

Maud taught us how to play the recorder. ☐

There is no need to be disagreeable about this. ☐

The day passed uneventfully and we were all bored. ☐

It was so hot that Roy unzipped his coat. ☐

arm	armed	disarmed	☐
cuse	excuse	excused	☐
tract	retract	retractable	☐
match	matched	mismatched	☐
place	replace	replacement	☐

The cops disarmed the bank robbers. ☐

We were excused games because it was freezing outside. ☐

My dad uses a craft knife with a retractable blade. ☐

Jake wore mismatched socks today. ☐

If that torch is no good, you should ask for a replacement.☐

out, found, our, loud, house, about, sure, sugar

hunk   hurl   hurt

If you burn your hand, it is sure to ___.

urge   fur   arm

Did it hurt when I twisted your ___?

sump   sugar   sunk

At our house, we make rice pudding with ___.

curve   card   car

We got a very good price for our ___.

teen   teeth   three

She is sure to need a brace on her ___.

end   eat   eke

That is the third cake that you are about to ___.

out   our   oat

If you tell a big fib, you are sure to be found ___.

barn   barge   bark

Our dog has black fur and a loud ___.

☐ Pass: 10 sec.   ☆ Bonus: 8 sec.   ★ Double Bonus: 6 sec.

bake	railed	brick	wishful	☐ ☆ ★
gloat	nuke	torches	snake	☐ ☆ ★
call	hoard	Luke	thickest	☐ ☆ ★
runt	chick	softly	trick	☐ ☆ ★
chicken	joist	bloke	bashful	☐ ☆ ★
pike	parting	yoke	bairn	☐ ☆ ★
stuck	soppy	link	quake	☐ ☆ ★
ball	eke	helpless	green	☐ ☆ ★
Dick	clack	replay	sharpest	☐ ☆ ★
predict	wall	unseen	wake	☐ ☆ ★
board	sent	batten	tend	☐ ☆ ★
hack	joint	unjust	broke	☐ ☆ ★
before	soapy	hoarding	drain	☐ ☆ ★

Neal, the Real Seal.

Mark did not want to stay in the boiler room with Sue, the gruesome stoker. It was hot and dirty in the boiler room, and coal dust got up his nose. So he said to Sue, "I cannot shift coal with tea in my boots. I must go and find a pair of socks that are clean and dry."

Sue said, "That is just fine, but make sure you come back quickly. It is time to stoke the flames with more coal, or the boiler will run out of steam and this trawler will not go."

So Mark ran up the stairs to the next deck. He ran up more steps until he reached the fresh air. There on deck he tripped on a pail of raw prawns.

"Watch out," a voice barked, "Small boys should look where they go. I am Neal, the real seal, and I am in charge of sorting raw prawns."

Mark said, "I am Mark, a small boy who is six, and I must find the mess decks or Maud, the maudlin trawler woman, will be cross with me. I should be washing the dirty dishes. Can you tell me how I can find the mess decks?"

Neal, the real seal said, "By now, Maud is crying into her tea again, so you can help me sort prawns. You must put the small prawns into this pail, and the large prawns go in that pail."

Mark asked, "What do you do with the small raw prawns?"

Neal said, "I eat them, because real seals need lots of prawns."

So Mark sat down and started sorting prawns. Raw prawns do not smell very nice, and real seals do not smell so good, too. But it was better than shifting coal with Sue, the gruesome stoker. When he had sorted out his first pail of raw prawns, Neal, the real seal tipped it into his mouth and ate them in one gulp.

"Now that was just fine," said Neal, smacking his lips. "You sort out a very nice pail of prawns."

Mark asked, "Why do they call you a real seal? Are there many fake seals about?"

Neal looked at Mark shrewdly. "There are lots of fake seals. Seals are very cute, so everyone wants to be a seal. No one will like you if you are cruel to a cute seal. But we can't have fake seals eating all the raw prawns." Then Neal looked around and said, "I can see dark clouds to the west. There is a squall coming. We must put these prawns away and close the hatches. We do not want this trawler to sink in a storm."

Split Digraph

hope	those	ride	theme	write	nine	☐
lines	slate	blade	knife	twine	plane	☐
state	chime	tune	spine	slide	Pete	☐

I hope we can go on those rides at the theme park. ☐

You must write nine lines on the slate. ☐

Sharpen the blade of the knife and it will cut the twine. ☐

I would not fly on a plane that is in such a bad state. ☐

Those chimes play a nice tune. ☐

Pete hurt his spine going down the slide. ☐

Crete	globe	Jane	like	glide	ice	☐
skate	mule	tame	smile	grade	Dane	☐
nude	cone	scope	drape	gripe	gale	☐

Can you find Crete on the globe? ☐

Jane likes to glide across the ice on her new skates. ☐

I think that mule is tame. ☐

Smile if you got good grades! ☐

Do Danes like to swim in the nude? ☐

Would you like an ice cream cone? ☐

DECODING ⚡ POWER ⚡ PAGE

Remember to practise the flashcards at least once a day!

thwack	scrumpy	splutter	strapless	☐
male	bemuse	skate	spiteful	☐
dewy	cruelly	fewer	strew	☐
preclude	dislike	shrunken	scrunches	☐
awe	staunchly	redrawn	gauntest	☐
expose	became	wisely	useful	☐
stripe	preshrunk	thrip	splitting	☐
awning	maudlin	defraud	dawned	☐
prideful	unsafe	shameless	unmade	☐
Tuesday	strew	hewn	clueless	☐
Jane	wifely	beginning	exclude	☐
thwaite	sprayed	thrush	sprightly	☐
bulge	brace	squirl	grunge	☐
unfailing	smartly	prepay	throaty	☐

Wordbuilder

Always use the cursor!

pair	repair	repaired		☐
spot	spotless	spotlessly		☐
screw	unscrew	unscrewed		☐
card	discard	discarded		☐

I just had my watch-strap repaired, but it broke again. ☐

When Joyce has cleaned the house, it will be spotless. ☐

Mike unscrewed the lid on the jar. ☐

Pete discarded all that useless junk. ☐

spell	spelling	misspelling	misspellings	☐
plode	explode	exploded	unexploded	☐
main	remain	remaining		☐
join	joining	adjoining		☐
force	forceful	forcefully		☐

Jane was unhappy about all her misspellings. ☐

You must stay away from that unexploded bomb. ☐

There are just six sweets remaining in the jar. ☐

Dawn and Maud slept in adjoining rooms. ☐

Floyd made his point very forcefully at the meeting. ☐

old, cold, hold, both, most, were, once, only

spam   spring   Spain

Sue once flew to ___ in her nice new plane.

cokes   colds   cones

We both caught our ___ from Dawn.

hurt   hurry   happy

Paul and Joyce were both ___ in the crash.

bone   both   boat

Please hold onto the rail with ___ hands.

fate   fault   frail

It is not my ___ that we are late.

only   once   old

Next year, Jade will be nine years ___.

knew   new   grew

Most of our friends ___ where we were.

bed   grass   stew

I like to watch the snakes crawl in the ___.

☐ Pass: 10 sec.   ☆ Bonus: 8 sec.   ★ Double Bonus: 6 sec.

explore	suck	flair	beset	☐ ☆ ★
aimless	dismiss	joke	frail	☐ ☆ ★
explain	drake	unpick	boxes	☐ ☆ ★
refund	fairer	prevail	juke	☐ ☆ ★
shore	unfit	daft	reject	☐ ☆ ★
pluck	coast	prevent	Mike	☐ ☆ ★
expel	thankful	between	joined	☐ ☆ ★
distress	choke	jeer	express	☐ ☆ ★
rainy	bemoan	shake	steep	☐ ☆ ★
refrain	catch	quick	judge	☐ ☆ ★
marches	etch	prevent	coyly	☐ ☆ ★
fridge	flake	tight	unwell	☐ ☆ ★
Ray	itch	begin	hedge	☐ ☆ ★

The Storm.

Up on the bridge, Nate, the First Mate blew a mighty blast on his horn, and the crew of the trawler came running out on deck. The black clouds in the west were drawing closer and the sky grew very dark. The crew were stuffing raw prawns in lockers and coiling up all the ropes. They were folding up deckchairs and reeling in washing lines. Mark did not have a clue what to do. Neal, the real seal, was barking out orders to the crew when the first drops of rain fell. A cold wind blew in from the west and Mark was cold, wet and dirty. He was still black with coal dust.

"At least this rain will rinse me clean", he said to himself.

Then the squall struck, and the wind tore the sea into a white froth. Huge waves tossed the trawler around and Mark had to hold tight to a rail. Should he go down to the boiler room and help Sue, the gruesome stoker? At least he would not be cold there. But what if the trawler sank? Mark did not want to be trapped down below.

Then Neal, the real seal, came up from behind and slapped his back with a flipper. "Come with me, my boy, you will be safe on the bridge. Even if this rusty old trawler sinks, you can hold onto me, for seals can swim very well."

So Mark went with Neal, the real seal, up to the bridge. The trawler pitched and rolled, and Mark almost lost his grip. A huge wave almost swept him into the sea, but Neal saved him just in time. Neal still smelled of raw prawns, but Mark held onto him just the same.

Up on the bridge, Maud was still crying, and she had no big mug to drink from, for a change. Nate, the first mate, clung to the wheel and steered the rusty old trawler up and down the huge waves. Nate barked orders to the crew, as only an old sea dog can. He had drained the water from his pipe and was trying to light it, but no smoke came from his ears.

Neal, the real seal, said to Mark, "Now you can be a real sailor. The port lookout has just turned green. Go and be lookout for him. If you see anything but water, you must report it to me."

ue, ew

Always use the cursor!

shrew	chew	Sue	blew	jewel	☐
Kew	true	yew	value	knew	☐
clue	dew	new	Lew	cue	☐

Can a shrew chew hard cheese? ☐

The wind blew Sue's boat back to shore. ☐

How many yew trees did you count at Kew Gardens? ☐

What is the true value of these jewels? ☐

I knew that Lew would not have a clue. ☐

There was some dew on the new grass this morning. ☐

threw	screw	blue	gruel	Sue	☐
fluent	Lew	glue	drew	few	☐
crew	cruel	grew	flue	due	☐

Nate threw a few screws into the blue tin. ☐

We had to eat some thin gruel for lunch. ☐

Sue can speak French fluently. ☐

Lew drew a few sketches. ☐

The crew grew restless waiting for the tide. ☐

It is cruel to put glue in the locks. ☐

DECODING ⚡ POWER ⚡ PAGE

Do not award ticks for a 'good try'—your pupil will pay for it later!

broadly	cloying	bestir	refloat	☐
screw	newest	shrewd	clue	☐
shrill	squawk	strap	thresh	☐
unwise	brainy	expertly	dismay	☐
thaw	redrawn	tawdry	awning	☐
strewing	airless	doleful	audit	☐
ensue	hoarding	straining	slightly	☐
screed	before	boastful	chewing	☐
painless	shrew	awe	flaunted	☐
cheese	brightest	hugely	drunken	☐
switching	skirmish	bewilder	murky	☐
enrage	curly	darkest	gravely	☐
ewe	rice	sorely	flightless	☐
script	throbbing	bespoke	spawn	☐

Wordbuilder

Remember to practise the flashcards at least once a day!

reck	reckless	recklessly	☐
plug	unplug	unplugged	☐
lax	relax	relaxing	☐
mand	demand	demanded	☐

Boy racers like to drive recklessly. ☐

Be sure the toaster is unplugged before you try to fix it. ☐

Faith likes to play relaxing tunes. ☐

The greedy girls demanded new bikes. ☐

treat	treated	mistreated	☐
mast	dismast	dismasted	☐
tract	extract	extracted	☐
pain	painless	painlessly	☐
drink	drinkable	undrinkable	☐

The nasty boy mistreated his pet snail. ☐

They treated the dirty water to make it drinkable. ☐

The sailing boat was dismasted in the squall. ☐

Luke's rotten teeth were painlessly extracted. ☐

My dad's home-made wine is undrinkable. ☐

old, cold, hold, both, most, were, once, only

cold   cost   Coke

Is there space in your desk for me to hide my ___?

mine   mike   mill

Shall we meet at your place or ___?

bird   birth   birch

When I am nine years old, I will ask for a pet snail for my ___day.

hold   most   dawn

Shall we get up at ___ and watch the sun rise?

swam   walked   flew

Grace and Bruce both ___ to Greece last year.

once   only   done

Hurry up—there is ___ one seat left!

fridge   flames   frames

If your hands are cold, hold them near the ___.

sludge   gunge   gum

Most of my friends were chewing ___.

FLUENCY READING

rake	high	needful	might	□ ☆ ★
lodge	display	all	light	□ ☆ ★
Luke	batch	expand	point	□ ☆ ★
fudge	unstuck	night	smoke	□ ☆ ★
eke	badge	fetch	often	□ ☆ ★
right	reset	failing	pitch	□ ☆ ★
puck	ridge	prefix	croak	□ ☆ ★
sight	exact	ditch	thankless	□ ☆ ★
hatch	betray	thinner	nudge	□ ☆ ★
shack	fight	disrupt	fleet	□ ☆ ★
thatch	hutch	large	resit	□ ☆ ★
mice	take	firm	bridge	□ ☆ ★
richest	burst	prepaid	huge	□ ☆ ★

The Rocky Shore.

Mark was proud to have a real job, but he was afraid too. Mark was now the port lookout and he could just see over the rail. As far as he could see, there was only water. The cold spray hurt his skin and he had to squint to see in the driving rain. The rusty old trawler creaked and groaned as it pounded into the waves. Mark wished he was back in Bart's shack with Vern and Froid. He wished he was with Hank, the hunch-backed horse, who was a real mate, or with Jake, the fake snake, in his rusty old junk cars. At a pinch, even Mike, the loan shark, would do. Maybe he could have changed into a witch at the church by the strange bridge, where Smudge, the batty cat with a flat cap, lived. But it was no good wishing that he had not gone fishing. He hoped that Neal had a good home to take him to.

Mark was almost dreaming when he saw some lights. He yelled to Neal, the real seal, who came running over as fast as his flippers would go.

"Look over there!" Mark pointed to the lights.

Neal took out his spy-glass and looked at the lights. "Why, that is land over there. If the wind forces us on to the rocks, this rusty old trawler is done, and so are we."

Maud told Nate, the first mate, who gave up trying to light his pipe and threw it over the rail. They looked at the lights and at last Nate said, "That must be the rocky shore of Bangalore. If we can't get more speed out of this tub, it will smash on those rocks."

Maud said, "We need more steam if we are to get away from the rocky shore. Someone must go and help Sue, the gruesome stoker. She must have help shoveling coal into the boiler."

But no one wanted to go below. No one wanted to be trapped in the boiler room when the trawler hit the rocks.

Maud said, "I must stay by the wheel and steer this ship, so I cannot go below."

Nate, the first mate, said, "I must stay and bark at the crew, so I cannot go down to the boiler room."

Neal, the real seal, said "I cannot shovel coal because I cannot hold a shovel in my flippers."

At last Mark said, "There is no point in looking out because we know exactly what is there. I will go below and help Sue shovel coal."

 ....

Mastery Test

If your pupil does not pass this test they must go back to page 129. This is very important—a child who is struggling will not be learning. Contrary to what you would think, most children would rather go back than carry on getting things wrong. If your pupil needs to go back, use a different coloured pencil for ticking the boxes.

Use the cursor as you would on a Fluency Reading page.

Timed reading: 'Pass' mark is 15 seconds per line.

cue	slate	unsafe	maudlin	☐
boasting	crew	scope	useful	☐
redrawn	value	gripe	chewing	☐
tune	airless	sprayed	blew	☐

Reading accuracy: Pass mark is one mistake.

Do not prompt. You may allow your pupil to self correct, but you cannot say anything except "Try again".

Nate threw a few brass screws in the blue box. ☐

Those new chimes send a chill down my spine. ☐

June helped me plant a few yew trees from Kew Gardens. ☐

If Lew will sharpen the blade, Dawn will cut the twine. ☐